CHEAPER TACKLE

Cheaper
Tackle

———

ROBERT BRUCE

WITH 133 DRAWINGS

LONDON
ADAM & CHARLES BLACK

FIRST PUBLISHED 1960
REPRINTED WITH MINOR CORRECTIONS 1966
BY A. AND C. BLACK LTD
4, 5 AND 6 SOHO SQUARE, LONDON, W.1

*To my Parents
in gratitude for their
patience*

PRINTED IN GREAT BRITAIN BY
THE CAMELOT PRESS LTD., LONDON AND SOUTHAMPTON

CONTENTS

INTRODUCTION

I WAS seven years old, and feeling low. It was a Saturday morning and a glorious summer's day and there was available trout fishing, only two miles from home. My bike was ready, but though I longed to go fishing I could not overcome the fact that I was short of tackle and, as usual, short of money!

As I sat by the fireside some twenty odd years later I remembered the occasion with a rueful smile and gradually the idea of this short book grew into being. How many just such young and enthusiastic anglers there must be, who meet the same problems of costs of tackle replacement. Thoughts of the innumerable hours of happiness I have had at the waterside prompted me to compile the following chapters on tackle-making at home.

The book is primarily intended for the young angler with definitely limited funds to meet replacement costs.

Over the last twenty years or so I have spent many hours on river banks, trying and hoping to convince trout and other varieties of fish that my lures were the real thing! Inevitably a proportion of these hours has been fruitless, as regards catching fish, but not one of them has been other than a source of pleasure and contentment. I began fishing at the ripe age of six years, and of a height so meagre, that, on river banks with tallish undergrowth, only my rod was visible to a by-stander. I owe any knowledge I have of fishing to my Father, and it is through him that I learnt how many pleasures are to be had from fishing, as well as the thrill of catching fish. Certainly the objective of a day's fishing is to catch fish, but to be able to enjoy the open countryside and view Nature's treasures with an eye of appreciation and an understanding of some of her signs is a tremendous source of happiness and contentment.

I sometimes think that if all the world were anglers, then strife and war would cease; there would be no time for them!

In these early outings my height was such that, though I was constantly invisible to the fish, I was equally constantly managing to tangle cast and line in the growth all around me! Truly I found at a very early age, that tackle losses could be heavy, and even worse, that replacement costs were prohibitive to one of my financial state. Whereas my sixpence pocket money would then buy one fly cast, I found that I could manage, without any trouble, to lose two or three casts in a day's fishing, let alone a week! Also, it was soon apparent that in the well fished waters near home, the best results were to be obtained by deliberately fishing the more inaccessible and therefore, least fished spots. Alas, the result of this policy was invariably further tackle losses, soon of a frequency, such that my youthful finances were exhausted!

Obviously the problem of costs needed serious thought, if I were to continue as a budding angler. So we come to that Saturday morning at an age of seven years, when I resolved to make as much of my tackle as possible, for as little as possible. Over the years since then, various items have been made and tried, each having two major objectives:

1. Cheapness
2. Deadliness

The easier the tackle was to make, and the commoner the materials required, the better. When I think back on how my earliest efforts must have upset my Mother's tidy home and my Father's ideas on bed-time, I marvel at their patience.

Gradually, however, various items of tackle were evolved with much financial improvement. As my skill as an angler slowly increased to more normal levels, my tackle losses became less frequent, and I was again able to have my fishing outings, limited only by time factors, and not by financial ones.

My Father taught me first, wet fly and later dry fly fishing, and consequently my early effort at tackle making revolved around cheaper flies and casts. Later I was introduced to the art of spinning, and so entered the tackle field of spinners and traces. At one stage, I even tried my hand at rod making by way of two of my Father's old wooden shafted golf clubs. The result may not have been as elegant as a factory produced spinning rod, but it was the means by which I could afford to spin for four or five seasons. Gradually over the years I made many different items, and though a lot of them had to be discarded as impracticable or not effective, I have tried to collect together those items of tackle which have proved, throughout the seasons, to be deadly and yet can be made easily at home, and very cheaply.

I hope the descriptions will help the reader to avoid some of the many pitfalls that I seemed unusually able to find! It is interesting, that over the years I have had so much pleasure from tackle making that even those items I could now afford to buy, I still make at home. There is a great satisfaction in seeing the job build up before your eyes and by your own efforts, and how much greater the thrill of catching fish with your own home-made lures. I now spend many a happy winter's evening stocking up the tackle box in preparation for the next season's sport (and losses). I continue, as usual, to suffer tackle losses each year but no longer is my fishing limited because of tackle costs.

Many readers will no doubt know of, or devise, better methods than those described in the book, but if some of the ideas here result in a few young enthusiasts being able to fish oftener and with added pleasure, then the objective of the book will have been fulfilled.

—and so to battle with soldering iron, and pliers, for longer, better and cheaper fishing——!

CHAPTER I

BASIC EQUIPMENT

IT is assumed that most young anglers keen on home manufacture of tackle are owners of a certain amount of basic and essential gear. Some may be fortunate enough to own equipment suitable for several different types of fishing, but many intending tackle makers will own equipment suitable for one type of fishing only. Possibly some young enthusiasts are just collecting the necessary gear for fishing, and below, briefly described, are several average, but essential, outfits for different types of river fishing. Indications are given as to which items are best bought and which can be made at home. Needless to say, those items which are suggested as being best bought are best to be bought in the highest quality that can be afforded. Some points in choosing such equipment are mentioned, and it is hoped that these remarks will assist the young angler in gathering his basic gear together as cheaply as possible, yet of high quality and suitable for the type of fishing intended.

The items which are suggested as being bought are those it is impossible to make at home, within the objective of this book, i.e. cheaply and easily. Thus, only the more skilled, who own a full range of tools, including several especially for the job, will find rod making possible. Similarly as regards rods, there is nothing superior to high quality split cane, and to make a split cane rod at home is a major and time consuming task. No, for the majority of anglers, certain items will have to be bought, and unfortunately rods are the major item. Although the initial outlay on such an item may seem high, the fact that a high quality rod will give a lifetime of trouble free fishing makes the cost, in fact, very reasonable.

Rods

Fly Fishing

The rod is, of course, essential, and the angler who can but afford one for both wet and dry fly fishing is strongly urged to buy one built specially for dry fly. Such a rod can perfectly well be used for wet fly fishing, whereas a wet fly rod is never suitable for dry fly fishing.

The young angler needs a light and reasonably short rod, which is easily handled, nicely balanced and of course of lasting reliability. Most will find that an 8-foot to 8-foot-6-inch rod is of best all round use, and those of medium trouting weight will, with experience, be found to be able to cope quite adequately, even with salmon. Split cane of reputable make is by far the best material, but is unfortunately one of the more expensive. An 8-foot-6-inch rod of high quality and of well known make can be obtained in N.E. England now for £6 6s. A lot of money?—not really, considering that this rod has given me steady service for the past fifteen years, and remains as good as ever: a cost of 8s. 6d. per season; not unreasonable!

Regarding other materials used in rod manufacture, the only other suitable alternatives are, greenheart, steel, or glass fibre. Greenheart is appreciably heavier, and has not the snappy action of split cane, also it is much more liable to breakage. Steel and glass fibre are fairly light, but again haven't the snap in their action as has split cane.

All, however, are cheaper than high quality split cane, and will give many years of perfectly good service. In each case it is probably wiser to buy a slightly heavier grade of rod to obtain comparable action to split cane, and in the case of greenheart, a rod 9 feet long is really needed.

The rod rings in dry fly fishing are best to be of the agate type at the tip and butt of the rod, and of the full ring type in between. (Fig. 1.)

The number of sections to a rod is a debatable point. Ideally, a one-piece rod gives the best action, but obviously in all but exceptional circumstances, its length and vulnerability while being carried, make this inadvisable. An 8-foot to 8-foot-6-inch rod can be easily carried in two sections and this gives a much nicer action than that of a three-section rod of similar length. The butt is best to be made of cork, shaped to fit the hand grip, but please, make sure it is of large

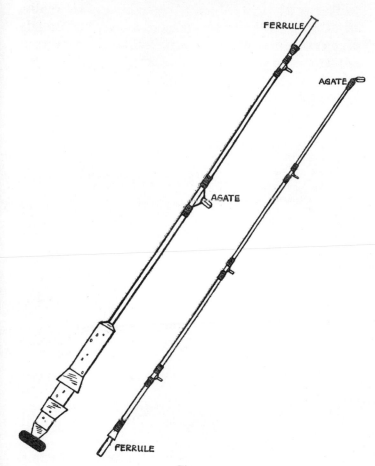

FERRULE

AGATE

AGATE

FERRULE

Fig. 1

enough diameter to grip comfortably. Many tend to be of slightly small diameter and can be quite tiring to hold at the end of a day's fishing.

The reel seat should of course be freely adjustable and made of non-corroding metal, preferably one of the many light alloys. There are two common patterns, both perfectly adequate (Figs. 2 and 3), although the pattern in Fig. 3 gives firmer seating to the reel.

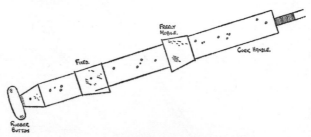

Fig. 2

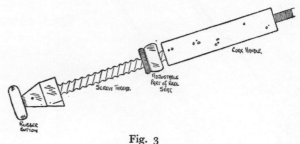

Fig. 3

The ferrules can be of either the normal suction type or of the locking variety. Good quality suction ferrules never give trouble, if reasonable care is taken of them, and they are lighter and less liable to jam than the locking type.

Here then is the suggested rod: 8 foot to 8 foot

6 inches long, of split cane, two sections, suction ferrules, cork handle, reliable reel seat, and of medium trouting weight.

All prospective buyers for the first time, are urged to take an experienced angler with them, for guidance regarding appropriate weight and action of the rod. Always erect the rod, attach the reel and line you intend using and TRY ITS ACTION in the shop, before buying. The action and balance that suit one angler, do not necessarily please the next one, and rod-buying is largely an individual choice.

Of course, different rivers and conditions may warrant considerable variation on the above, which is merely suggested as a starting point in considering choice and type. A young angler can obtain information about local conditions and needs from seasoned anglers of the district, and adapt his choice accordingly.

A rod, as above, and of first class quality, will cost £6 6s. and last a lifetime. Cheaper qualities and other materials can result in perfectly satisfactory rods costing as little as £2 10s. although such rods will not last so long.

If you are lucky enough to buy a rod for wet fly fishing separately, then a longer rod with a softer action is indicated. Whereas, the dry fly rod has a relatively sturdy tip and a snap in its action to flick cast and fly forward and backward; the wet fly rod can be much more soft and gentle (almost wobbly) in action as it has to merely

B

propel the cast and flies, not dry them also. Because of the softer action, the wet fly rod is better to be 9 to 9½ feet long, so as to be able to pick up, and throw, a reasonably long line. A rod of this length will be found easier and safer to carry if in three sections, rather than two and as there is less shooting of line through the rod rings in wet fly fishing, the need for agate butt and tip rings does not arise. Split cane is lightest and gives longest trouble free service, and can be made so as to give the appropriate softer action. Greenheart and glass fibre are also used, but again, Greenheart is heavier and more prone to breakage; glass fibre is perfectly satisfactory.

If a rod of greenheart is purchased, remember, the point of major importance is that the grain of the wood must run closely, evenly and straight along, the length of the rod. Wood grain running obliquely across the rod spells future disaster in the form of breakage, and a rod with such grain should be avoided at all costs, as it is never cheap at *any* price.

Spinning

The earlier remarks about materials apply equally to spinning rods, and split cane is again best, though glass fibre or greenheart can be perfectly satisfactory. For most spinning, a 7-foot rod in two sections and of medium trouting weight will provide best all-round service. Prior points about ferrules also apply here, but the butt of the rod should be long enough to accommodate

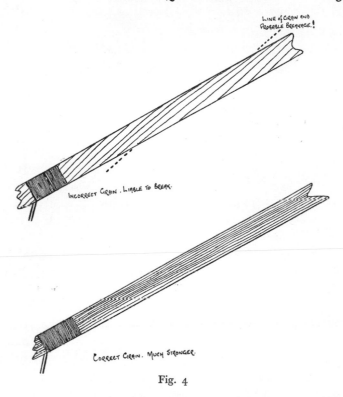

LINE OF GRAIN AND PROBABLE BREAKAGE!

INCORRECT GRAIN. LIABLE TO BREAK.

CORRECT GRAIN. MUCH STRONGER.

Fig. 4

both hands and the reel, in comfort. Both parts of the reel seat should be freely mobile, so that the reel position can be varied to suit the balance of the rod in one-handed and two-handed casting. Rod rings are best if of the stand-off type, and should all be of agate or similar hard materials. The butt ring should be about 1-inch internal diameter to allow for the side to side movements of outgoing line when casting.

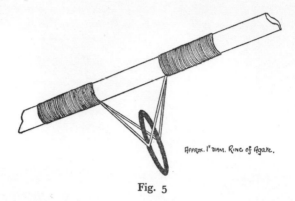

Fig. 5

Bait Fishing

Frankly, I have never been interested in tournament fishing, and consequently my bait fishing has always been done with either my fly rod or, more usually, my spinning rod. Since the advent of the fixed-spool reel, threadline technique of fishing, I have always used my spinning outfit. However, for those who desire a rod specially for bait fishing, I would suggest one 9 feet 6 inches to 10 feet long, in three sections. The bottom two sections should be of good quality whole cane and the top section of split cane or greenheart. The rod's action is required to be virtually all in the tip section, hence, for lightness, whole cane is eminently suitable for the lower two sections. A long two handed butt with a firm reel-seating mechanism is needed, and stand-off type rings, the tip and butt ones being of agate. Often, such tournament rods are sold with two tip sections which are interchangeable. From a personal point of view, I have always felt that the expense of such a rod for normal bait fishing is unnecessary, and I find my spinning outfit quite adequate.

Reels

These again, unfortunately, need to be bought. Price varies with type and size, but first-class fly-fishing reels of $2\frac{1}{2}$ inches to 3 inches diameter in light non-rust alloy, can be obtained for £2 0s., and will last for many years. A word about the ratchet of such a reel however. This device is a necessity, its main use being the prevention of overrun (due to the angler or a hooked fish). The ratchet should be adjusted so as to allow line to be pulled from the rod and reel with firm tension, but not so firm as to cause breaking of the cast. The tension needed should be sufficiently LESS than the breaking strain of the cast, to allow for sudden jerks on the line, since no fish is going to considerately apply the tension gently!

Spinning reels are a more expensive item, but well worth their cost. There are many varieties on the market, but the fixed-spool threadline type are best. The price range is tremendous, but a reel such as the Mitchell Pattern is very reasonably priced, of first-class quality and has the advantage of two line-drums, easily interchangeable, one for trout and one for salmon fishing.

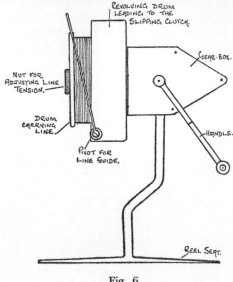

Fig. 6

Lines

Fly-fishers require a line which balances in weight with the rod's action, and for most river fishing should be 20-30 yards long. It should be made of non-twisting material and impervious to water. The best is doubtless plaited silk with a good line dressing to make it waterproof. Should the line absorb water it swells, increases in weight, sinks in the water when cast, and becomes more and more difficult to control, pick up from the water and shoot out, at each subsequent cast. My feeling is that a high-quality line is an expense more than worth while, and with care, a good line will give many seasons of service. An added but useful refinement is a tapering end to the fly line. The line in the last few yards gradually tapers down to an appreciably thinner grade at the very end.

Both ends of the line can be dealt with in this manner, so that the line can be reversed after a few seasons, if the end becomes frayed or weakened with use. Such an arrangement certainly allows slightly longer casts to be made, and enables the flies to be presented to the fish much more delicately.

One well known make of line, with both ends tapered, costs £3 3s., but I have used mine now for eight years and it is still perfectly reliable, so that, again, the apparently high initial cost is more than justified. However, adequate and quite satisfactory lines can be bought from 18s. upwards and the angler's pocket will be one of the decisive factors determining choice. Using a rod as previously described for dry fly fishing, I find the medium trout or H grade of line correct for my rod's action and balance, but all buyers are well advised to try the reel with line on the rod before buying, to confirm that the balance is right.

Spinning

Here we find a cheap and capital substance for lines in nylon and its fellow substances. Nylon is light, elastic, thin yet strong and is waterproof.

Moreover, it does not rot. Nylon lines can be bought in various lengths and strengths, and any reputable make is perfectly satisfactory. It is best to buy at least 50 and preferably 100 yards, in one filament. If of, say, 4-lb. breaking strain, 100 yards will cost 6s. to 10s. Pretty cheap for many seasons of fishing! As I mentioned before, I find my spinning line first-class for bait fishing also. The strength of line bought will vary with the average fish weight expected and the finesse of the angler's technique, along with local conditions and circumstances. I use 4-lb. breaking strain for trout and 6-lb. breaking strain for salmon, but obviously this will not be suitable for everyone, and each angler must decide for himself; if a novice, after obtaining advice from a local veteran!

The above items are the basic ones needed for the commoner types of river fishing and, as can be seen, the cost can be reasonable with very satisfactory results, or it can be as high as the angler cares! It is, however, sound advice to stick to reputable makes, and to buy as good quality as can be afforded, such equipment will repay itself over and over in the course of the years.

Equipment such as casts, artificial minnows and so on have not been mentioned as, in later chapters, I hope to describe how many of them can be made at home and so serve as a pleasurable winter's hobby, and as a source of cheaper yet deadly tackle.

CHAPTER 2

FLY-TYING

BEFORE discussing methods, it's just as well to briefly consider the theories behind fly-fishing with artificial lures. On gazing into tackle-shop show-cases of flies, there are two main impressions: the incredible number of flies of different size, shape and colour combinations, and the remarkable cost of a small hook with coloured feathers attached! Despite the glorious array of colour in the tackle shops, there is no doubt that the major part of the colour scheme is wasted, as far as the fish are concerned! If an artificial fly is floated on the surface of a glass of water and the reader views that same fly through the bottom of the glass, only an object in shades of grey is seen. The colour can be as vivid as one cares to imagine, but to the fish under the water the probability is that the fly is seen as a black or grey silhouette in which shape, size, and manner of presentation are far more vital than colour schemes in persuading the fish that the artificial is the real thing! It seems pointless therefore in paying for intricate colour schemes if they are of little value from the angling point of view.

Far, far more vital are size and shape of the artificial fly. Obviously a hatch of flies on the river over the course of one day will result in flies of mainly one size and shape, but in the evening, or on other days, a different variety of fly or moth may result in a hatch of flies bigger or smaller and of completely different shape to the earlier hatch. It becomes important to the angler, therefore, to know the commonly found flies, on his stretch of water, and also to know roughly at what times in the season the various flies usually appear.

The colours of the individual flies don't much matter, more should he note the size and shape of the flies and their usual way of travel downstream (i.e. on the surface or submerged).

Viewing the tackle-shop selection of flies again, the reader will soon realise the savings involved if he can make his own flies. Dry flies, for example, commonly cost 1s. to 1s. 6d. each! Considering the ease with which three, four or even more can be lost in a day's fishing, it isn't hard to imagine why I began to make my own flies to ease the expense burden! In the methods described below, the finished flies have been tried for several years and have proved as deadly as the bought variety, but they cost about 1d. instead of 1s. to 1s. 6d. each.

Materials

Pair of fine-pointed scissors (Mother's!).
1 doz. size 14 long-shanked eye hooks (9d. to 1s.).
Piece of candle or, preferably, beeswax.
Small vice, preferably a pin vice (2s. 6d.).
Selection of feathers (see below).
Selection of thin thread (Gossamer, Silko, etc.).

Let's take the above in turn. The scissors are best if of the embroidery type with about $1\frac{1}{2}$-inch blades. Most mothers have a pair and can be persuaded to lend them, as only feather and thin thread will be cut with them. The important thing is that they must have fine, sharp-pointed blades.

Any smallish pair of scissors will do the job, but the type shown in Fig. 7 makes the job easier.

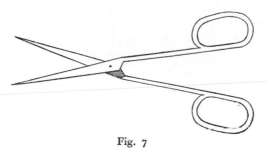

Fig. 7

The hooks should have fairly long shanks of fine gauge, with a well-finished, down-turned eye. The barb should, of course, be needle sharp, as should the point of the hook (Fig. 8).

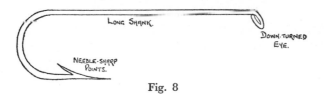

Fig. 8

The candle or beeswax is used to coat the thread before use, so as to make it handle easily and lie snugly round the hook. Beeswax can be

obtained from the local saddler's shop for about
2*d*.

The vice used can be of standard type with
jaws about 1 inch to 1½ inches across, but far
better is a pin-vice, which will cost 2*s*. to 3*s*. 6*d*.,

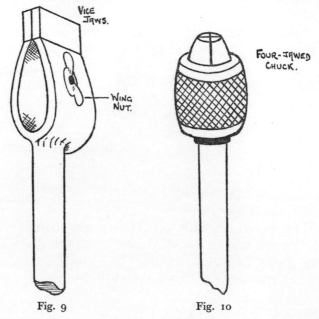

Fig. 9   Fig. 10

depending on the type. They can be obtained
from hardware and ironmongery shops, and two
of the commoner types are shown in Figs. 9 and
10.

The vice needs to be fitted with a clamp to
hold it on to the edge of the work bench or, as I
use it, held with the stem of the pin-vice in the
jaws of a normal small vice.

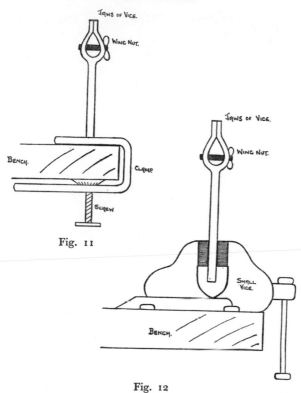

Fig. 11

Fig. 12

Feathers are not difficult to obtain if word is passed around friends and relatives, especially before Christmas and New Year festivities! The feathers mostly used are those $1\frac{1}{2}$ inches to $2\frac{1}{2}$ inches long, with stiff, springy, shiny hackles, from the throat of the bird. Which bird? Well by far the most useful is the common cockerel. Colour can be varied to suit one's inclinations, but Rhode Island red is very useful, also white, black and dark fawn. Other birds such as duck, pidgeon, guinea-fowl and snipe are all useful sources of different colour and texture and size.

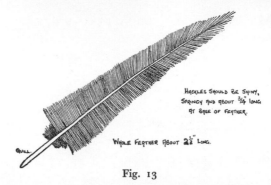

HACKLES SHOULD BE SHINY, SPRINGY AND ABOUT ¾" LONG AT BASE OF FEATHER.

WHOLE FEATHER ABOUT 2½" LONG.

QUILL.

Fig. 13

It is always worth getting a few of the shorter wing feathers (2 inches to 3 inches long), matching feathers from each wing.

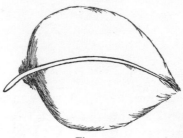

Fig. 14

It is surprising how obliging friends will be, once they realise what you are looking for, and the main problem soon becomes not how to get suitable feathers, but where on earth to keep them all! The most useful feathers for size and shape are shown above (Figs. 13 and 14), but many others can be utilised by an enterprising enthusiast.

During my first few seasons at fly-tying I used my Mother's embroidery Silko threads exclusively, with perfectly satisfactory results! However, for 1s., bobbins of gossamer silk can be bought which make a rather neater job. Colours should be strictly limited and I use almost only fawn, black, yellow, white and red.

A bobbin of thread ties innumerable flies, so that, per fly, cost is infinitesimal.

Added, though not essential requirements, are spring clips to keep the thread taut while fly-tying, a spool of golden or silver thread tinsel for glisten effect and a piece of peacock feather. The latter can sometimes be obtained from Mother's wardrobe if any ancient headgear has been stowed away in an odd corner, otherwise it will cost 6d. or 1s. to buy at the tackle shop.

Method

First, general principles

You require a comfortable seat with good lighting directed on to your work table. It is best to sit towards the right-hand end of the table, with the vice firmly clamped about 1 foot from the table end, so that there is space, to the left of the vice, on which to lay out the various items to be used.

Always keep all hooks, other than the one in

the vice, in a clearly labelled and safely closed tin box. It can be a great tragedy to have a child, or pet dog, find a hook on the floor and either have it stick in their foot or even swallow it, so please take this sensible and so simple precaution.

Below is a sketch of a typical artificial fly that we will set out to make.

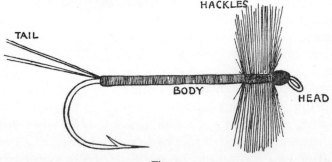

Fig. 15

This type of fly is the easiest to make and a most useful all-rounder.

Place a hook in the pin-vice as in the diagram, and close the vice so that it is firmly held, with the shank well clear of the top of the vice jaws and no part of the point of the hook projecting beyond the side of the vice jaws (Fig. 16).

Now unwind about 12 inches of black thread from a bobbin, and thread the loose end through the centre of the bobbin so that the end of the thread can be held, with the bobbin hanging down without more thread unwinding. Stroke down the length of thread one or two times with the beeswax so that it shows no tendency to coil.

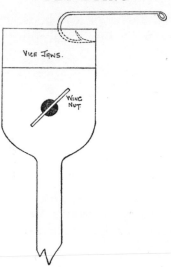

Fig. 16

To start the body of the fly, place the thread along the shank of the hook and hold it with the thumb and forefinger of the left hand as in Fig. 17.

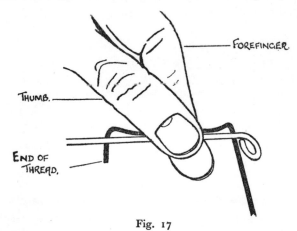

Fig. 17

C

Wind the thread four to six times round the hook shank as if starting a whipping (see Fig. 18)

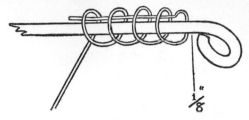

Fig. 18

including, with the shank, the short end of the thread. Make sure, however, that the first turn of thread lies at least $\frac{1}{8}$ inch behind the eye of the hook.

Hold the long end taut with the right hand and stroke the short end remnant up so that it stands up from the hook shank. Transfer your left hand to the long end of the thread and, keeping it taut, snip off the excess of the short end with your scissors in your right hand (Fig. 19).

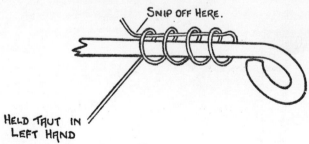

Fig. 19

Continue winding thread round the shank so that one turn lies snugly against the next, until the

turns extend as far as the point *just before* the
shank begins to curve to form the hook.

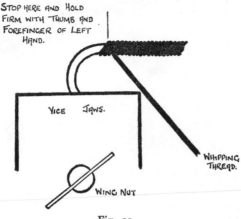

Fig. 20

The time for the first knot has arrived! Hold
the last turn of thread round the shank with
thumb and forefinger of the left hand, so that it
does not uncoil, and with the right thumb and
forefinger spin the long end of thread between
finger and thumb, so that it curls up into a loop.
With a little practice, it becomes remarkably
easy to make this loop rear up in front of the eye
of the hook and slip on to the hook shank (Fig.
21).

Pull this loop loosely round the hook shank
and then ease it along the shank with the forefinger nail of right hand, till it lies at the end of
the previous turns of thread, and there pull it
firm. The prior waxing of the thread makes this

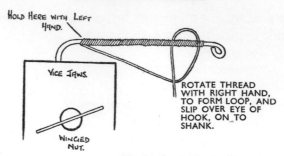

Fig. 21

simple half-hitch bite quite sufficiently to hold firm (Fig. 22).

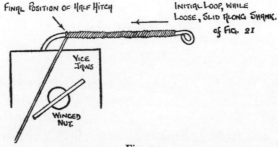

Fig. 22

Let the thread and bobbin hang loose and choose the feather for the tail of the fly. The tendency is to take far too much feather for this; what is needed is two to four single hackles about ¾ inch long and no more. Let's take a ginger-coloured feather 2½ inches long from a cockerel. Tease off three or four hackles as in the diagram (Fig. 23), pulling them away in the direction of the thick end of the central strand of the feather with thumb and forefinger.

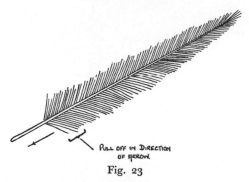

Pull off in Direction
of Arrow.

Fig. 23

Now moisten the quill end (previously attached) of these hackles between your lips just
enough to keep them all lying together. It is best
to pull them off the feather with the left hand as
they are now to be laid along the top of the hook
shank, so that the ends that were attached to the
centre of the feather lie over the last few turns of
thread on the hook (Fig. 24).

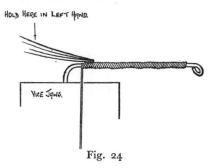

Hold Here in Left Hand.

Vice Jaws.

Fig. 24

Holding them so, with thumb and forefinger of
left hand, with the right hand make a few turns
with the thread round the shank including the
ends of the hackles. Make these turns of thread

lie snugly one in front of the other, working back towards the eye of the hook (Fig. 25).

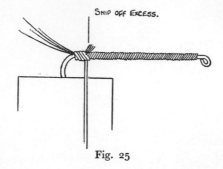

Fig. 25

Holding the last turn taut, with the thumb and finger of the left hand, snip off any excess feather with the scissors. Now continue winding thread round the shank, turn against turn, till you reach a point about halfway along the hook shank. Using the same technique as before, slip a loop

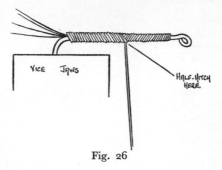

Fig. 26

on to the hook shank so as to form a half-hitch knot and pull firm, just in front of the last turn of thread.

The novice will almost certainly find it necessary to have a few practice runs at these steps. I certainly did! The annoying thing is to find all seeming to go well, and then too much tension is put on the thread, it snaps, and you've to go back to the beginning again! Don't be discouraged if this happens; you rapidly learn just how much tension to apply to the thread to pull the turns and knots firm without breakage. I would strongly advise the reader to practise thus far first, and master this seemingly small point before carrying out the next steps, as it is very discouraging, to say the least, to have the thread snap when the fly is virtually completed!

We've now come to the point where the hackles are inserted. The type of hackle feather used decides whether the fly is to float (dry fly) or sink (wet fly). For a dry fly, pick out a feather (ginger again) about $2\frac{1}{2}$ inches long with short, shiny, springy side shoots about $\frac{1}{2}$ inch long. A wet fly requires softer hackles about $\frac{3}{4}$ inch long with little springiness in them, but, again, on a feather about $2\frac{1}{2}$ inches long. Prepare the feather by stroking gently with thumb and forefinger down both sides from tip to base, so that the hackles stand out at right angles to the central strand. Pull off the last few hackles on each side and stroke the feather so that the very tip hackles lie separated from the rest, as in Fig. 27.

Hold the feather about its centre in the left hand and moisten the tip hackles with the tongue so that they lie closely together. Now place the

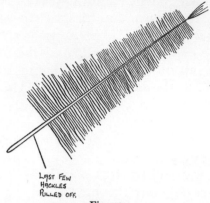

LAST FEW
HACKLES
PULLED OFF.

Fig. 27

feather along the top of the hook shank so that the
tip hackles lie just to the right of the last knot in
the thread.

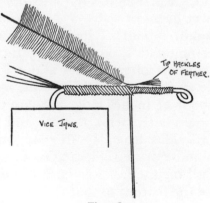

TIP HACKLES
OF FEATHER.

VICE JAWS.

Fig. 28

Make a few turns with the thread, working
towards the eye, round the shank and tip hackles
and then make a further half-hitch knot as in

Fig. 29. Snip off any excess feather. Continue winding forwards to a point $\frac{1}{8}$ inch behind the

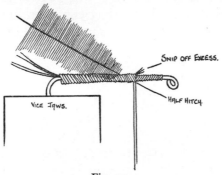

Fig. 29

original starting-point and again tie a half-hitch, as explained before.

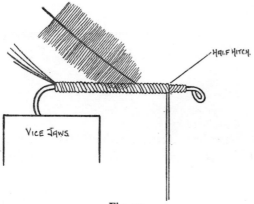

Fig. 30

Let the bobbin of thread hang loose and gently lead the thread out at an angle to the right of the hook's eye, and let the bobbin hang over the bench end. This is merely to move the thread out of the way of the next manœuvre, and any means of anchoring the thread without damage to it, will suffice, e.g. hang it over a nail projecting from the table edge (dotted line in Fig. 31).

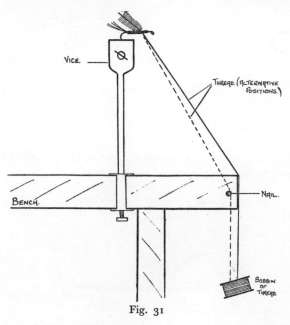

VICE.

THREAD. (ALTERNATIVE POSITIONS.)

BENCH.

NAIL.

BOBBIN OF THREAD.

Fig. 31

Place the left hand behind the hook and the right in front. With the left thumb and forefinger, pull the end of the feather round the back of the shank and feed it through to the right hand, between the vice and diverted thread. Continue the movement round the front of the hook shank with the right hand to the top, where again the left hand takes over, and so on. The object is to whip the feather round the hook, winding one turn slightly in front of the other, towards the eye. *Note that the vital point is to wind the feather round the shank, so that the hackles stand out at right angles to the hook shank,* and that this means winding the

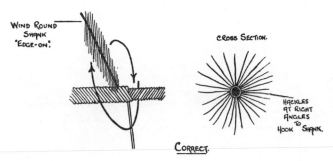

Fig. 32

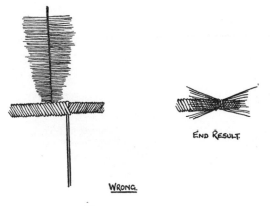

Fig. 33

feather on "edgeways" as it were, and not in the apparently obvious flat way.

Having wound the feather as far forward as

the last knot the only tricky part has arrived. Hold the feather taut with the *right* hand underneath the shank and, with the *left* hand, stretch under the hook and pick up the thread and bobbin and pull it under the shank of the hook to the left of your right hand (Fig. 34).

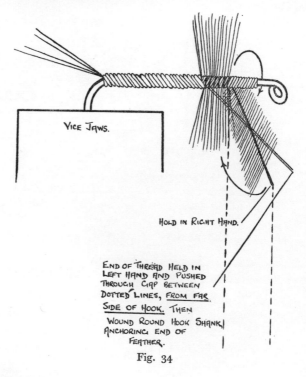

VICE JAWS.

HOLD IN RIGHT HAND.

END OF THREAD HELD IN
LEFT HAND AND PUSHED
THROUGH GAP BETWEEN
DOTTED LINES, FROM FAR
SIDE OF HOOK. THEN
WOUND ROUND HOOK SHANK
ANCHORING END OF
FEATHER.

Fig. 34

Still with the left hand, pull the thread taut from the front and wind it over the top of the shank so that this turn of thread lies just in front of the last turn of the feather, but includes, in its turn, the feather end, still held in the right hand. At this point a stage is easily found where, by keeping the thread taut with the left hand and pulling gently in a direction away from the fly-tier, the right hand can be relaxed and the feather end continues to be held firm by this last two-thirds turn of the thread (Fig. 35). Using the

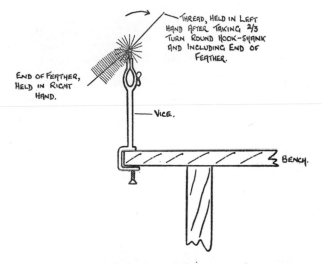

END VIEW WITH HOOK HELD IN VICE.
Fig. 35

right hand and keeping the thread taut, complete the turn round the shank and add three or four more, almost up to the original starting-point (Fig. 36), and, as described earlier, apply two half-hitch knots round shank *and* feather end (Fig. 37).

Let the thread hang loose again and, *avoiding*

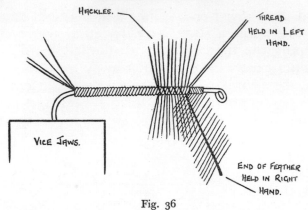

Fig. 36

cutting the thread!, snip off the excess of feather end still protruding.

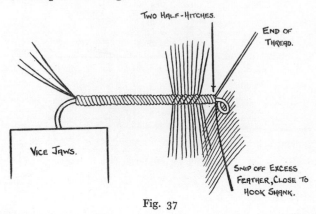

Fig. 37

Finally, with the thread (uncut, I hope!) take a few further turns round the shank up to the base of the eye and finish off with three or four half-hitches.

A point to note is that if Silko thread is used the

final knots will prove bulky, and it is as well to place the last two knots on the underside of the shank, in the angle made between shank and eye, where they are less noticeable. Snip off the thread close to the last knot, and there is your first fly!

Using this knotting technique, I have never found any need to lacquer the "head" of the fly so as to keep the knots from working loose, but I would advise gossamer silk be used, if possible, to get a much neater finish.

And there it is!

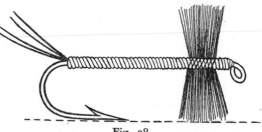

Fig. 38

It may be desirable to trim the fly a little because of misjudgement or unsuitable hackle length. The hackles should stand out like the spokes of a wheel in a stubbly, compact collar round the shank and be of a length so that they reach from the shank as far out as the hook point. If they are longer, they can simply be trimmed with scissors. The tail piece should sit cockily up and back, above the curve of the hook, and be about ½ inch long, and can be trimmed accordingly.

Many dry-fly faddists, I know, will be aghast at my feelings on colour and on trimming the hackles. But why does a fly float, anyway?

It's a question of surface tension supporting the hackle tips and being sufficient to carry the

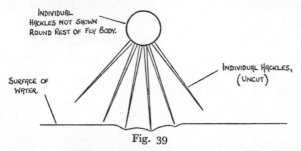

INDIVIDUAL HACKLES NOT SHOWN ROUND REST OF FLY BODY.

SURFACE OF WATER.

INDIVIDUAL HACKLES, (UNCUT)

Fig. 39

weight of the hook. Now, normal individual hackles come to a fine point, with a consequently extremely small point of contact with the water.

If the hackle tips are trimmed there is a slight

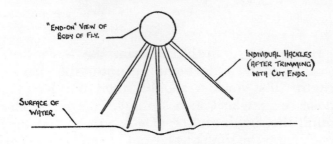

"END-ON" VIEW OF BODY OF FLY.

SURFACE OF WATER.

INDIVIDUAL HACKLES (AFTER TRIMMING) WITH CUT ENDS.

SHOWING "DIMPLING" DUE TO SURFACE TENSION WHEN FLY FLOATS ON THE SURFACE.

Fig. 40

increase in the area of contact and thus slightly greater support.

I cannot believe a fish can spot this minute degree of difference, and certainly the fly, if anything, will float even better!

As regards colour schemes—well, that's up to the angler, the area he fishes and the materials available. I find the patterns listed at the end of the chapter extremely useful and quite as deadly as more precisely copied shop versions of flies.

I feel certain that it is much more to the point to have a selection of *sizes* of flies, on, say, hooks of size 14 mainly, a few on hooks size 12 and 10 and one or two on size 16, rather than to worry about colour. The reader is no doubt wondering why no mention has been made of winged flies. I'm afraid I am again at variance with many faddists, as I do not feel they add at all to the deadliness of the lure, and they most certainly add to the difficulties of home manufacture!

As regards tinsel (gold or silver) or quill bodies for flies, I employ the following simple additional steps:

When the stage of tying in the tail is reached, along with the tail feathers, in my left hand I hold the end of the tinsel thread and proceed to tie in both together (Fig. 41).

After tying in with the thread and winding the thread forward to halfway along the shank, instead of next inserting the hackle, I take the tinsel thread and wind it round the shank, working forwards to where the thread finishes. I then make a half-hitch with the thread round the

D

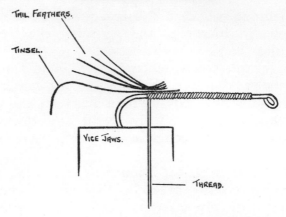

HOLD TAIL FEATHERS AND TINSEL IN LEFT HAND.
Fig. 41

shank and include the tinsel in it and then snip
off any excess tinsel (Fig. 42).

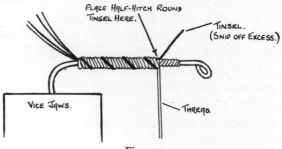

Fig. 42

Whether the turns of tinsel are wound one
against the other or widely apart can be varied
according to the angler's wish. Thus, in the case
of a Greenswell's Glory, I usually place four
separate turns round the shank between the tail

and starting-point of the hackle. The fly is then completed as before, inserting the hackles, etc. (Fig. 43).

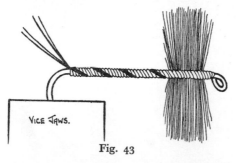

VICE JAWS.

Fig. 43

Quill bodies are made using exactly the same technique, but the quill part is derived from peacock feather. One "hackle" about $2\frac{1}{2}$ inches long is pulled from the feather. The fuzzy outer layer is carefully and gently scraped off, using the thumb-nail against the forefinger and drawing the hackle gently between them. There is left the central strand which has a variegated greenish colour, one half dark and the other an olive colour.

This quill is then tied in with the tail, as was the tinsel, and similarly wound forward and again anchored, as was the tinsel. Each turn of quill should lie snugly against its neighbour, so as to obtain that pleasing, finely striped effect, of a segmented insect's body. The quill is more delicate than the thread so that the reader is well advised to go extra carefully and gently when tying this type of body on to the hook.

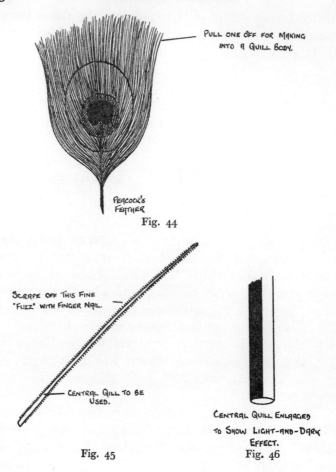

PULL ONE OFF FOR MAKING
INTO A QUILL BODY.

PEACOCK'S
FEATHER

Fig. 44

SCRAPE OFF THIS FINE
"FUZZ" WITH FINGER NAIL.

CENTRAL QUILL TO BE
USED.

Fig. 45

CENTRAL QUILL ENLARGED
TO SHOW LIGHT-AND-DARK
EFFECT.
Fig. 46

In the case of making wet flies, I use exactly the same technique, but use longer and softer hackles, using feathers from the lower part of the bird's throat. The end result is shown below (Fig. 47), and the hackles are stroked backwards slightly towards the point of the hook and left rather longer.

There are many modifications of style, colour,

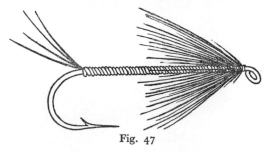

Fig. 47

shape and size that can be tried, according to the reader's ideas and all the steps described can be

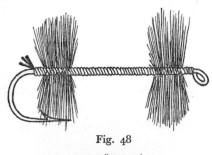

Fig. 48

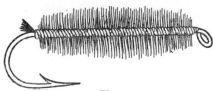

Fig. 49

varied in their sequence to obtain the desired effect.

Thus, two hackles can be tied in as in Fig. 48,

or one long stubby hackle used, to give a grub effect (Fig. 49).

Or a whole feather can be tied in for a streamer effect on a single hook, or Pennel or Stewart tackles (Fig. 50).

Fig. 50

Tails can be altered to be stubby and fat, long, or merely absent!

There are infinite variations to be tried if the angler wishes, and he can be literally prepared for all water conditions by dint of careful selection and choice of shape and size. The colour schemes I leave entirely to suit his own views! I have included at the end of the chapter, however, a typical selection of flies that I carry with me on a day's fishing of uncertain conditions. It may prove of some help, I hope, for a young angler, in starting his own collection of lures.

A final word about cost: the overall cost runs at 1*d.* to 1½*d.* per fly, and by tying flies in the winter evenings, in preparation for the coming season, not only is the cost a fraction that of bought flies, but the reduced cost is also spread out through the winter months in small amounts and the angler at the same time has a most pleasurable hobby to pursue out of the fishing season! Results with the flies listed below have proved quite as good as with bought flies over many seasons now, and I am sure the young reader will find new delight in catching fish with his home-made lures.

Suggested Fly Patterns

1. Ginger tail
   Red body
   Ginger hackle
2. Ginger tail
   Red body with four turns of gold
      tinsel
   Ginger hackle
3. Fawn tail
   Olive body with four turns of gold
      tinsel
   Medium brown hackle
4. Black tail
   Red body
   Black hackle

} 4 very useful "all-rounders"

5. White tail
   Black body } Useful dusk fly
   White hackle
6. Fawn tail
   Yellow body
   Ginger hackle
7. Ginger tail
   Quill body
   Medium brown hackle
8. Brown tail
   Yellow body with four turns of gold tinsel
   Black hackle

9. Ginger tail
   Gold tinsel body } Useful if water slightly coloured
   Ginger hackle

Remember, the size of hook used should be varied to suit local conditions.

CHAPTER 3

ARTIFICIAL SPINNERS

SPINNING lures must prove lifelike to the fish if they are to be successful. A popular minnow used today costs 3s. 6d. to 4s. 6d., according to size, and, considering that an angler can lose three or four in a day's fishing, the cost can, in a season, prove prohibitive!

Several years of experimentation resulted in the minnows described below. These minnows have proved to be deadly lures, easy and cheap to make and, very important, extremely effective in avoiding underwater snags. Considering that the cost per minnow works out at 7d. to 8d., even an occasional loss doesn't cripple the bank balance!

Materials

Sheet brass, $\frac{3}{64}$ inch thick, 3 inches long, 2 inches wide.
Modeller's brass tubing gauge 10, 12 inches.
Bicycle valve rubber, 12 inches.
String of old beads about $\frac{1}{8}$-inch diameter (assumed obtainable free from feminine quarters!).
Size 14 treble hooks with eyes, one dozen.
One dozen size 11 swivels.
2 to 3 yards nylon of 6-lb. breaking strain.
Quick-dry lacquer paint, 3 small tins (blue, green, white).

It is anticipated that handymen at home will already own the following necessary tools:

Soldering iron, flux and solder.
Vice, file, two pairs of small pliers, hacksaw.

The above materials are sufficient for one dozen 1-inch minnows.

Method

Hold the brass sheeting in the vice and with the hacksaw cut it into one dozen pieces $\frac{3}{4}$ inch long and $\frac{1}{4}$ inch wide (Fig. 51).

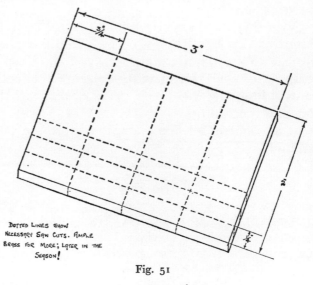

DOTTED LINES SHOW NECESSARY SAW CUTS. AMPLE BRASS FOR MORE; LATER IN THE SEASON!

Fig. 51

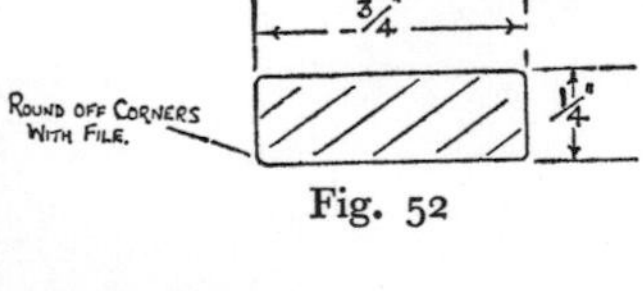

ROUND OFF CORNERS WITH FILE.

Fig. 52

(If it is possible to obtain brass strip $\frac{1}{4}$ inch wide, then the job is much easier; cut a 9-inch length of it into one dozen $\frac{3}{4}$-inch long pieces.)

Round off the corners of the rectangular pieces with the file (Fig. 52).

These twelve pieces will form the propellers of the minnows.

Cut the brass tubing into 1-inch lengths (obviously, the length of individual minnows can be varied to suit local conditions).

Now take each piece of tubing and, holding it vertically in the vice, make a $\frac{1}{2}$-inch longitudinal cut down the centre from one end (Fig. 53).

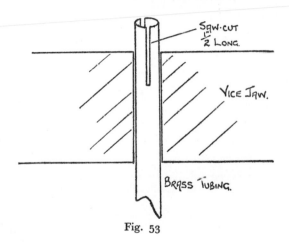

Fig. 53

Remove the tubing from the vice and smooth off all rough edges with the file.

Take one of the "propeller" pieces and hold it in the pliers as in Fig. 54. The objective is to twist each end leaving a flat, untwisted central part.

The central flat portion should equal, in width, the diameter of the tubing, so that the propeller can be fitted into the slot in the tubing. Thus in Fig. 54 length (*A*) should equal length (*B*) and length (*C*), the diameter of the tubing.

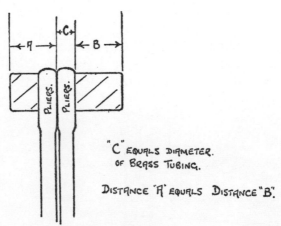

Fig. 54

Keep the central part flat with one pair of pliers and twist the other pair so that the brass is kinked through 45° in its long axis.

Repeat the process at the other end, again keeping the central area flat with one pair of pliers, making sure to kink the second end in the OPPOSITE DIRECTION to the first so as to give the propeller shape.

The whole thing takes a matter of seconds when expert at it, and can quite easily be done by eye.

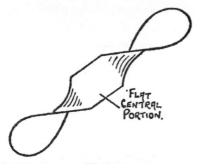

Fig. 55

Now slot the flat central part of the propeller down the cut made in the brass tube. In doing this the cut in the tube often requires opening slightly. If this is necessary, gently squeeze the tube back into shape with the propeller held firmly at the base of the cut.

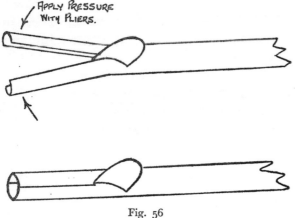

Fig. 56

Place a film of flux around the junction of the brass tube and propeller and solder into place.

If you are the fortunate owner of one of those small, light, electric soldering irons, the job is extremely easy. While soldering, hold the brass tubing in the pliers, NOT your fingers; brass is a good conductor of heat and a nasty burn can result if you use your fingers! It is only necessary to solder one side of the propeller to each side of the tubing.

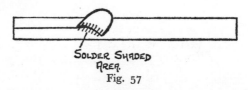

SOLDER SHADED AREA.

Fig. 57

When the solder is firm, file down any irregularities and then *simmer in boiling water for a few minutes*. This last point is important, as all flux is acidic, and any left inside the minnow will corrode the nylon used to attach the treble hook. I learned this the hard way by losing a fine salmon on its first run, simply because some residual flux had sadly weakened the nylon!

Next, cut off enough bicycle valve rubber to extend from behind the propeller to about $\frac{1}{16}$ inch beyond the end of the minnow's body. Moisten

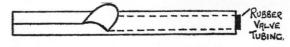

RUBBER VALVE TUBING.

Fig. 58

the outside of the rubber tubing and slide it inside the tubing as far as the propeller.

The rubber prevents fraying of the nylon on the end of the brass tubing.

The structure of the minnow is now complete, and it remains to attach the swivel and hook. I find the following arrangement very satisfactory:

Tie the swivel to the end of about 6 inches of nylon, using the Cairnton knot. Leave about $\frac{1}{4}$ inch of nylon after completing the knot (Fig. 59).

Fig. 59

Thread the long end of nylon through the minnow, from the propeller end, passing the nylon either above or below the flat central piece of the propeller inside the tubing.

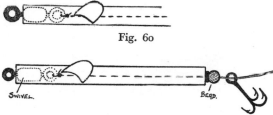

Fig. 60

Fig. 61

Pull the nylon through the minnow until the swivel lies two-thirds immersed in the nose of the minnow (Fig. 60).

Thread a bead on to the tail of the minnow, followed by a treble hook (Fig. 61).

To attach the hook I use the following knot
(Fig. 62):

Make two loops round the shank of the hook
and pass the free end of nylon back through both
loops. Draw the free end taut, so that the loops
are snugly, but NOT tightly, round the shank, and
the hook lies close to the bead and the swivel
lies in the nose of the minnow (Fig. 63).

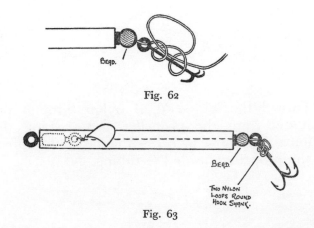

Fig. 62

Fig. 63

With a finger-nail, now ease each loop in turn
over the eye of the hook so that they lie between
the bead and the eye. Hold the hook's shank in
the pliers and pull the free end of nylon tight.
Next hold the hook with one pair of pliers and
the swivel loop with the other pair of pliers and
pull firmly, one against the other. This often
results in the taking-up of about $\frac{1}{16}$ inch of slack
and the end result should be as in Fig. 64.

Cut off excess nylon, leaving again about

$\frac{1}{4}$ inch beyond the knot, and there is your minnow awaiting a spot of colour!

For painting I used 6*d.* tins of quick-drying lacquer, blue or green for the top half of the

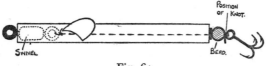

Fig. 64

minnow and white for underneath. I do NOT bother to paint on multicoloured spots, stripes or "eyes". If you study a spinning artificial minnow, it is quite obviously impossible for any fish to be able to tell the colour of individual spots or the "eyes"! All the colours blend into one overall hue, and I find blue and white or green and white adequate for all conditions.

Having painted the minnow, allow an hour or so to dry on some newspaper, and there is your completed minnow for the sum of 8*d.* and a little expenditure of time!

It's best to make the minnows in batches of, say, a dozen, making all the propellers at one time, then preparing the tubing, then the soldering and so on step by step. This way I find it a pleasant job that can be picked up during spare moments in the winter evenings.

A note about using the minnow is not out of place at this point. By all usual standards the finished minnow seems ridiculously light in weight. This is a distinct advantage in fact, since

E

any weighting that is required, can be added by using small split shot spaced along the trace $1\frac{1}{2}$ to 2 feet in front of the minnow.

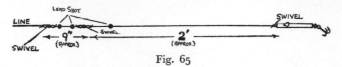

Fig. 65

The amount of lead used can be varied to suit the conditions and the depth at which you wish the minnow to run. Indeed, I find that by varying the weight and speed of retrieve it is possible to fish all areas, including stretches of water normally thought possible to be fished only with wet or dry fly.

The very lightness of the minnow well behind the weight of the trace is a distinct asset. It means that, on approaching an underwater snag, the minnow tends to swing wide of it, due to the water-flow past the minnow acting as a deflecting cushion (Figs. 66 and 67).

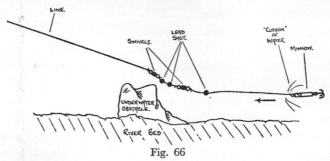

Fig. 66

Needless to say, it is far and away most satisfactory to use such minnows with a light rod and a

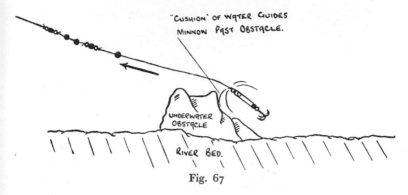

"CUSHION" OF WATER GUIDES
MINNOW PAST OBSTACLE.

UNDERWATER
OBSTACLE

RIVER BED.

Fig. 67

thread-line, fixed-spool reel, their respective weights being varied to suit the type of water, size of minnow used and size of fish anticipated. I use a 7-foot light split-cane rod with a 4-lb.-breaking-strain nylon line and 3-lb.-breaking-strain trace of nylon for trout and the same rod with a 6-lb. line and 4-lb. trace for salmon.

Minnows for salmon are, of course, considerably larger than those for trout, and a good all-round selection includes:

2 minnows	.	.	.	.	1 inch long
2-4 minnows	.	.	.	.	$1\frac{1}{4}$ inches long
2-4 minnows	.	.	.	.	$1\frac{1}{2}$ inches long
2 or 3 minnows	.	.	.	.	$1\frac{3}{4}$ inches long
1 or 2 minnows	.	.	.	.	$2\frac{1}{4}$ inches long

For the longer minnows for heavier fish, I use 8-lb. nylon for attaching the swivel and hook and a size larger in swivels and a treble size 12.

With the above selection you can be assured of many successful and, moreover, cheap days of fishing, along with a choice of minnows such as could not be previously afforded!

Minnow Tackles for Spinning

The tackle needed so as to be able to use real minnows for spinning is simple and cheap to make at home, and as minnows can be caught in number and preserved before the fishing season starts, such tackle is extremely useful and, moreover, very deadly. Spinning with such tackle is necessarily less convenient than spinning with artificial minnows, but it is, nevertheless, very effective and certainly cheaper!

The arrangement of the tackles can be altered to suit individual conditions, ideas, and minnow sizes, but the description below should provide a starting-point for the young angler from which to develop his own ideas:

Materials (for one dozen tackles)

Nylon of 6-lb. breaking-strain, about 4 yards.
Thin brass or preferably plastic sheeting 3 inches by 2 inches by $\frac{1}{16}$ inch.
One dozen size 14 treble hooks (eyed).
One dozen size 12 single hooks (eyed).
One dozen size 11 swivels.
One dozen small spring clips or loops.

Tools required are: Hacksaw, file, block of soft wood, a stout nail of about $\frac{1}{16}$-inch diameter, scissors, small pliers (two pairs), and a small hammer and a small metal vice.

Method

Let's make the "propeller" part first. Take the brass (or plastic) sheet and cut it with the hacksaw into pieces as shown in Figs. 68 and 69, while holding it in the vice jaws.

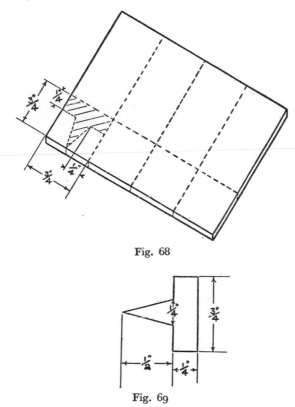

Fig. 68

Fig. 69

This is the most tedious part in making these tackles, but Fig. 68 shows one of the easier methods of cutting up the sheeting.

Having obtained these pieces, take each in turn and holding it in the jaws of the vice or with pliers in the left hand, round off the corners of the crosspiece with the file (Fig. 70).

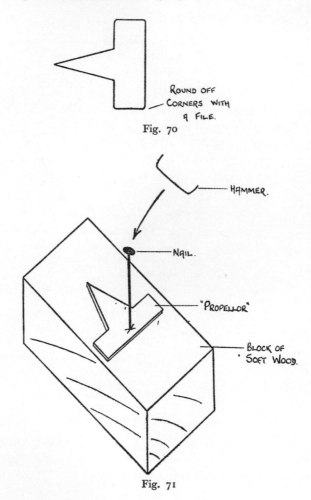

ROUND OFF CORNERS WITH A FILE.

Fig. 70

HAMMER.

NAIL.

"PROPELLOR"

BLOCK OF SOFT WOOD.

Fig. 71

Now place each piece, in turn, flat on the surface of the piece of soft wood, and with the nail and hammer pierce a small hole as indicated in Fig. 71.

The hole should be about $\frac{1}{16}$ inch in diameter and the edges should be smoothed off with the file. Take each piece in turn and, holding the central part of the crosspiece in the pliers, twist the ends of the crosspiece with the other pair of pliers, much as described in the making of artificial minnows. Again make sure to twist each end through about 45° in OPPOSITE directions, so as to give the propeller effect (Fig. 72).

Fig. 72

This then is the vital part of the tackle and it is merely a problem now of assembly.

Take about 9 inches of nylon and, using the knot shown in Fig. 73, tie on one of the treble hooks.

Snip off excess nylon, leaving about $\frac{1}{4}$ inch of nylon beyond the tightened knot.

Next fit one of the spring clips into the hole made in the "propeller" and fit a swivel on to the

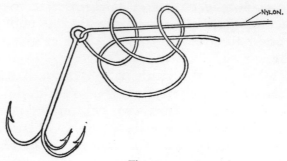

Fig. 73

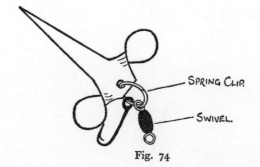

Fig. 74

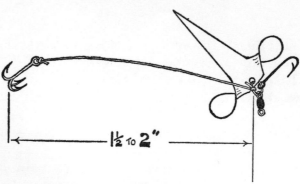

Fig. 75

clip and, finally, also one of the size 12 single hooks. This takes a little patience as the clip fills up, but is straightforward, the clip behaving like a miniature key-ring (Fig. 74).

Take up the end of nylon tied to the treble hook and thread it through the spring clip, and again tie the knot as in Fig. 73, adjusting the length of nylon between treble hook and spring clip so as to suit the size of minnow intended to be used (usually about $1\frac{1}{2}$ inches to 2 inches).

This is the simplest tackle and proves quite effective in use. I use it as below.

The tongue of the propeller is pushed down the throat of the dead minnow so that the cross-pieces stick out at the angles of the mouth.

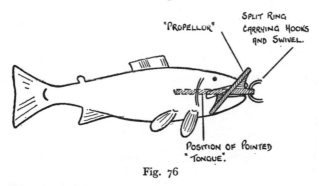

Fig. 76

Now take the single hook and firmly insert it into the shoulder region of the minnow, so that the full curve of the hook is buried. Lead the nylon along the side of the minnow and insert one of the hooks of the treble, very lightly, into the minnow, just in front of the tail fin, so that the hook picks up just enough thickness of tissue to keep it snugly in place at the side of the minnow's tail.

Here, then, is the minnow ready to attach to the

SINGLE HOOK INSERTED.

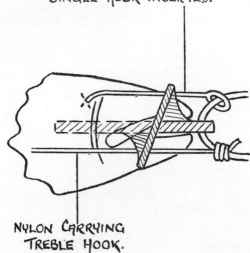

NYLON CARRYING
TREBLE HOOK.

Fig. 77

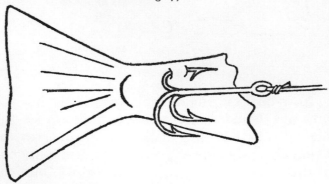

Fig. 78

trace. The reader, by experiment, may find that by imparting a slight curve in the minnow its spinning action is enhanced. This can easily be done by inserting the single hook first and then inserting the treble at a point so that the tail has to be pulled forward slightly to reach the treble hook.

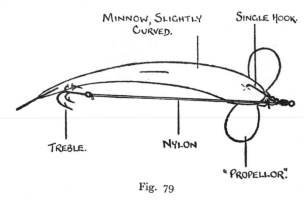

Fig. 79

A slightly more complicated tackle can be made as below which avoids the difficulty in making the above tackle an accurate length to suit the minnow used.

The materials remain the same, but the single hook, instead of being fitted to the spring clip, is looped on to the nylon as in Fig. 80. Remember to do this before tying the nylon to the spring clip (Fig. 80).

This arrangement allows the single hook to be slid along the nylon to a position suitable for insertion into the minnow's shoulder. This allows varying lengths of minnow, between $1\frac{1}{4}$ inches and

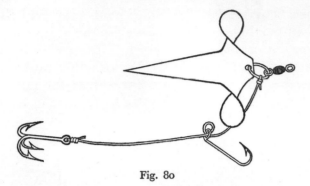

Fig. 80

$2\frac{3}{4}$ inches, to fit into the range of the one tackle.

I find that the sheet plastic gives a more easily worked and equally good propeller. It can be twisted to give the propeller effect merely by letting it soak in hot water a few minutes, taking it out and bending it with pliers to the required shape. It takes one or two minutes to harden in the new position, and there is your propeller. A note of warning: making the hole with a nail in the cold plastic is liable to crack it and it pays to heat the plastic a minute or two in hot water to soften it before driving the nail through; this should be done before twisting the ends of the cross-piece to form the propeller.

Many anglers like their spinning tackles to have two treble hooks attached. This is easily arranged to suit the anglers' taste as below:

Attach the spring clip and swivel to the propeller as before, and then attach a short piece of nylon, with another spring clip on its end, to the propeller's spring clip as in Fig. 81.

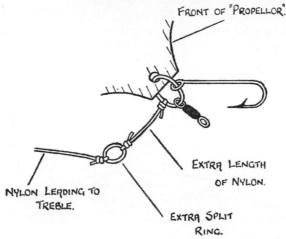

Fig. 81

The second spring clip should be about $\frac{1}{2}$ inch to $\frac{3}{4}$ inch from the first. The tackle is completed as before, after the extra treble hook is attached to the second spring clip (Fig. 82).

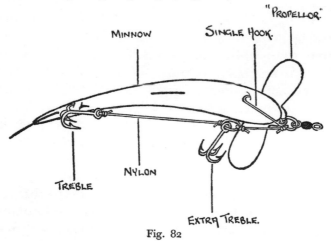

Fig. 82

In such a tackle the front treble hook can be used in place of the single hook or a single hook can be included in the second spring clip (Fig. 83).

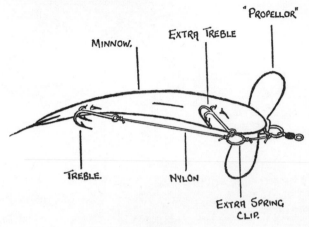

Fig. 83

I've always found it better to have one largish treble hook near the tail of the minnow rather than two trebles. If a fish takes a two-hooked lure, it is probable that both hooks will be inserted into different parts of the fish's mouth. This is anything but an advantage, since, if one hook is in the roof of the mouth and the other in the floor of the mouth, the fish on opening its jaws forcibly can use each hook as a lever against the other and may well dislodge both!

Also the line of pull can never be to the advantage of both hooks, so that either the hooking effect of only one treble is used (hence, why not

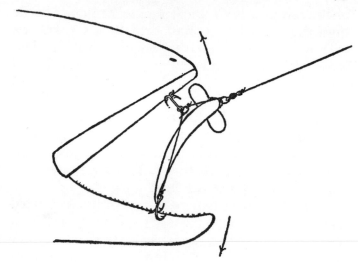

ARROWS SHOW DIRECTION OF PULL OF FISH'S
JAWS i.e. TEND TO PULL HOOKS OUT.

Fig. 84

just use one treble?), or the strain is taken by both trebles, both, however, being at a mechanical disadvantage.

Overall, then, I have always favoured a single-treble tackle, in conjunction with a single hook for keeping the minnow in place.

Such tackles as those described work out at about 4*d*. to 5*d*. each and are fished in the same manner as the previously described artificial spinners. Dead minnows do, however, weigh more, so that less lead shot will be required to weight the trace. Because most of the weight lies in the minnow itself, these tackles are more liable than the artificials to find firm "hook-holds" in underwater snags. Even so, the cost of the tackles is less, minnows can be caught when needed, and these facts compensate for the increased risk of loss.

There is no doubt that there are days when fish seem to prefer real, to artificial minnows, or vice versa, and an enthusiast will always carry a few of each type so as to be ready for any peculiar fancy on the part of the fish!

I usually carry two or three differently-sized tackles for minnow on a day's spinning, so that if the artificial proves non-productive, I can try with a real minnow. Needless to say, I also carry some thin nylon and a small single hook so that I can catch minnows as I need them, or I carry half a dozen or so carefully washed, preserved minnows, having removed them from the preservative the evening before and put them in a small screw-capped bottle. With a carefully chosen selection of artificial minnows and a few tackles for real minnows, and a small supply of minnows, the angler can confidently meet any spinning conditions at the waterside with the best possible chance of success. Regarding real minnow tackle, I usually carry the following in a small tobacco tin, along with the earlier suggested selection of artificial spinners:

Two 1½ inch from front spring clip to treble.
Two 2 inch   ,,   ,,   ,,
Two 1 inch   ,,   ,,   ,,

CHAPTER 4

CASTS, TRACES AND FLOATS

Fly Casts

CASTS for fly-fishing require to be long enough, and fine enough, to prevent a wary fish suspecting that any connecting link lies between the angler's line and his artificial fly! The necessary length in practice is about 9 feet, and a cast of this length of gut will cost the angler 3*s*. 6*d*. to 4*s*. 6*d*. Considering that one misjudged cast at the waterside can mean loss of the cast, the young angler is liable to find his fishing very expensive! Fortunately, nylon has proved a wonderful success and is relatively cheap. A spool of 100 yards of nylon will cost from 4*s*. to 10*s*., depending upon its thickness. A cast, therefore, works out at less than 4*d*. from a 10*s*. spool—quite a saving!

First, the reader must decide on the strength of nylon he requires. Most river fishing, other than salmon fishing, requires a cast of 3- to 4-lb. breaking strain, but the young angler is advised to govern his choice by local conditions, as these can vary widely.

The nylon on the spool has, of course, to be made up into individual casts, and below is described an easy and reliable method.

F

Cut off a 9-foot length of nylon from the spool, and at one end tie a double-knotted loop as in Fig. 85, so that the loop is about 1 inch long.

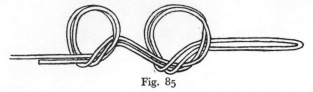

Fig. 85

For dry fly fishing there, then, is your cast! It could hardly be simpler, but please remember to tie the double knot shown; a single knot in nylon is very liable to slip.

For wet fly fishing a little more work is needed! After tying the loop as before, cut the 9-foot length into three 1-yard pieces. Now join them together again in turn, using the blood knot as shown in Fig. 86.

Each blood knot should be tied so that one of the ends is left about 3 inches long, the other end being cut off about $\frac{1}{8}$ inch from the knot.

This arrangement means that the complete cast has two knots in it, each with a non-sliding side-piece 3 inches long, suitable for attaching a fly. The final cast with flies attached should resemble Fig. 87.

Such a cast costs the angler, when proficient at the knots, about 4d.—plus five minutes in time! A 100-yard spool of nylon will provide the angler with thirty odd casts, enough for many days' fishing. A reliable and useful knot for attaching the flies to the cast is shown in Fig. 88.

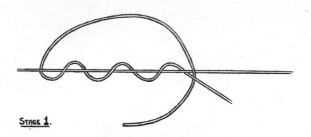

STAGE **1**.

STAGE **2**.

STAGE **3**.

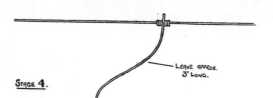

LEAVE APPROX.
3″ LONG.

STAGE **4**.

Fig. 86

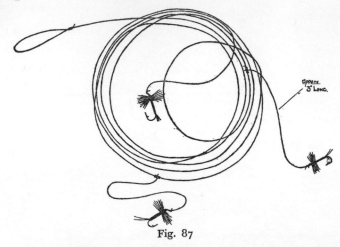

Fig. 87

A refinement in cast-making is to make the cast with a taper from loop to tip, so that the tip is the thinnest part. Such an arrangement is easy to fabricate, but means the angler must have a

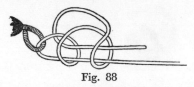

Fig. 88

selection of thicknesses of nylon. Instead of three 1-yard lengths, all the same thickness, join three of different thicknesses together, in exactly the same manner, each 1-yard length being one grade thinner than the previous one, working from the loop to tip of the cast.

Good results can also be obtained by making the loop and middle yards of the cast of the same thickness, and the tip yard a grade thinner. This lets the angler have a tapering cast, yet needs only two grades of nylon. Similarly, the dry fly cast can be built up and tapered, using three 1-yard lengths. In the case of a dry fly cast, however, the blood knots should have both ends of the nylon cut close to the knot, as only one fly at the tip is used (Fig. 89).

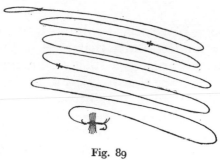

Fig. 89

Spinning Traces

For spinning, the angler requires a trace of a length largely determined by the length of the angler's rod! In order to be able to cast his lure accurately and afar, he must be able to swing his rod almost horizontally without risk to his minnow on undergrowth around him (Fig. 90).

The swivel attaching trace to line must be beyond the tip ring of the rod before casting, otherwise it is liable to jar and stick on being shot through the rod rings. These factors mean that a person of average height and using a 7-foot rod will find that a 3-foot trace is about as long as can be managed at the waterside.

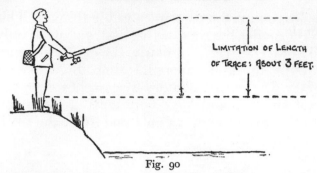

Fig. 90

In making the trace, it is important to make it of nylon a grade thinner than that of the line, so that if the minnow does stick on an underwater snag, it is the trace that breaks on pulling and not the line, since the line may break at a point many yards from the trace.

Two pieces of nylon are needed for the trace, and for trout fishing I use nylon of 3-lb. breaking-strain with a line of 4-lb. breaking-strain. From the spool of nylon, cut off a piece 9 inches long and a piece 2 feet 6 inches long. Two size 11 swivels are required, and the trace is made up by attaching a swivel to each end of the 9-inch length of nylon, and then the 2-foot-6-inch length of nylon to one of these swivels. The knot used is the same as that shown for attaching flies to a fly cast (Fig. 88).

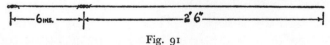

Fig. 91

The finished trace is shown in Fig. 91.

The short piece of nylon should be about 6

inches long after tying the swivels to it, giving an overall length of about 3 feet to the trace. The end swivel is attached to the spinning line and the minnow to the other end of the trace. In each case the same knot as before is used.

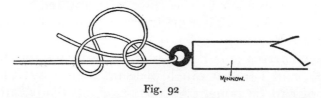

MINNOW.

Fig. 92

Of course, should the trace prove too long for local conditions on the river bank, the answer is to snip off a few inches of the trace before attaching the minnow. With longer rods and clear banks, the trace can be made longer or a further length of nylon attached to the one described, using the blood knot (Figs. 86 and 93).

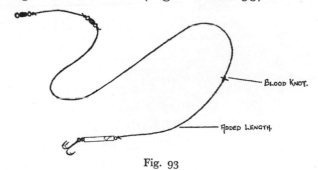

BLOOD KNOT.

ADDED LENGTH.

Fig. 93

As regards weighting the trace while fishing, I use common or garden split shot! For most spinning I nip on two shot of about $\frac{1}{8}$-inch diameter between the two swivels, and sometimes a third piece of shot about one-third of the way along the longer-length section of the trace. The number and size of the shot can be varied at the waterside to suit depth and currents of individual stretches of water. For several seasons, I used to nip the shot on to the trace with my teeth, but this is a bit unfair on the teeth (especially now, when I've only a few of the originals left!). I now carry a small pair of pliers with me for the job, and I find it much pleasanter this way! The shot can be bought for 6d. or 9d. all ready, and in varying sizes, in small metal boxes with sliding tops, very convenient for the pocket (Fig. 94).

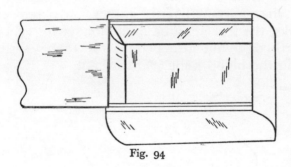

Fig. 94

Bait Casts

These are the simplest of all to make from nylon, again the strength of nylon used being varied to suit local conditions and size of fish. At home I use 2½-lb. breaking-strain nylon in casts of 1-yard lengths with my spinning outfit.

Cut off 1 yard of nylon and tie a loop about

1 inch long at one end, using a double knot as before. To the other end attach a single-eyed hook of appropriate size for local conditions. (Maggot fishers commonly use size 14 hooks.) The hook is attached in the same manner as a fly to the fly cast (Fig. 88).

Weighting of the cast is done with split shot, the shot nearest the hook being at least 9 inches from it.

A point about baiting such a cast with maggots: thread one maggot on to the shank of the hook, right up to the eye, and attach a second maggot to the curve of the hook by the tail end (blunt end!!) so that it is free to wriggle appetisingly. This arrangement hides the hook from the suspicious eye of the fish and looks like an extra large and juicy maggot specimen.

Many worm ("garden hackle") anglers prefer to use a two- or three-hook arrangement so as to prevent the worm from becoming bunched up in the water. There is no need to buy Stewart or Pennel tackles, as they are easily made at home with the materials you already have. Eyed hooks

Fig. 95

are a shade more conspicuous than non-eyed varieties, but the eye serves as a useful anchor for attaching the hook, and if properly baited the eye can easily be buried, out of sight, in the worm.

The eyed hooks are whipped on to the last 2 inches or so of the cast, each hook being about ¾ inch from its neighbour. Two or three hooks can be used, according to the angler's fancy.

Hold a hook in the pin-vice as when tying a fly (see Fig. 16) and thread the end of the cast through the eye of the hook so that the hook lies about 4 inches from the end of the cast (5 inches from the end if making a three-hook arrangement). Lay the end of some fly tying thread along the hook shank as in Figs. 96 and 97 and, starting at

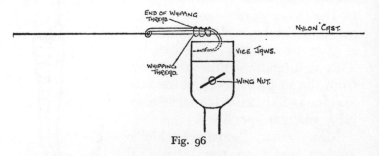

Fig. 96

the curve of the hook, commence whipping the thread towards the hook's eye, each turn of thread going round the shank, nylon and end of the thread. Each turn of the thread should lie snugly against the next, and it is useful to stroke the thread with beeswax as in fly-tying before beginning.

When about halfway along the shank, snip off the excess from the end of the thread and complete whipping up to $\frac{1}{16}$ inch from the eye.

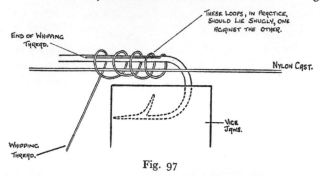

Fig. 97

Tie two half-hitches one after the other at this point, pull firm and snip off the excess thread.

Repeat the whole process with a second hook ¾ inch nearer the tip of the cast than the first hook, arranging things so that the second hook, when

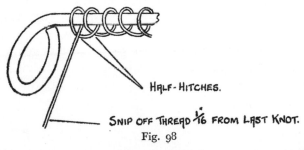

Fig. 98

whipped in place, lies on the opposite side of the nylon to the first. The third hook is tied to the tip, using the usual knot (Fig. 92), adjusting it so that when pulled firm the final hook lies about ¾ inch from the one above. Snip off the excess nylon.

The final result should look like Fig. 99 or 100.

In baiting such tackles with worms, it is best to

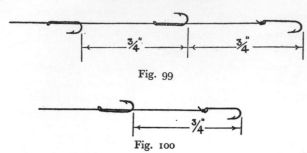

Fig. 99

Fig. 100

use bright red, frisky worms, about 2-2½ inches long. Attach the worm spirally as in Fig. 101, leaving ½ inch or so of worm beyond the tip hook to wiggle tantalisingly.

Floats

Many bait-fishers employ the float technique, and floats are quite expensive to buy, varying in price up to several shillings each. Fortunately they are simple and cheap to make at home.

Fig. 101

Materials

A few inches of thin copper wire (? Father's!).

A spool of black cotton (? Mother's!).

Several stout wing feathers from a hen (? Mother or neighbour!).

A few good quality corks about 1 inch in diameter (from local chemist at about 1d. each).

One of Mother's metal knitting needles.

Two small pots of quick-dry lacquer (dark green and yellow).

Small tube of waterproof glue.

Tools

Pair of scissors, small ordinary water-paint brush, sheet of fine sandpaper, razor blade, file, pair of pliers.

Method

Start by picking a cork with no cracks or fissures in it, and mark the centre of each end with a pencil (Fig. 102).

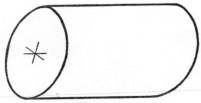

Fig. 102

Put Mother's knitting needle in the fire (when she's not looking!), leaving one end projecting over the edge of the grate and heat it to red heat. When glowing, pick it up by the projecting end with the pliers, held in the right hand. Hold the cork in the left hand between finger and thumb and carefully, with the needle, burn a whole through the centre of the cork, using the pencil marks as a guide. Before doing anything else, be sure, after burning the hole through the cork, to place the needle in a safe place to cool down, where it won't burn a hole in the carpet or furniture!

Now take one of the stout hen feathers and trim off all the hackles with the scissors as close to the central stem as possible. The residual hackle stump should be gently smoothed off with the fine sandpaper (Fig. 103).

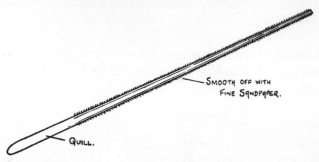

Fig. 103

Now cut the quill so that it is about 4 inches long, and be sure to cut off the excess from the *thinner* end. Insert the thin end of the quill into the hole in the cork and gently work it up and down till the cork jams firmly at a point about

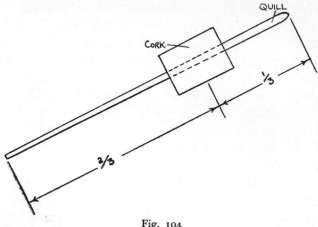

Fig. 104

one-third of its length from the thicker uncut end (Fig. 104). This stage may need a little further assistance from the red-hot needle to enlarge the hole a little. Care in selecting the needle size to be slightly less than the quill diameter, before starting, can save a lot of work at this stage.

The objective now is to round off the cork to a more professional-looking shape. With the razor blade, and holding the cork on an old piece of soft wood, trim carefully round each end of the cork as in Fig. 105. Work steadily round each end of the cork with small cuts, each overlapping the previous one.

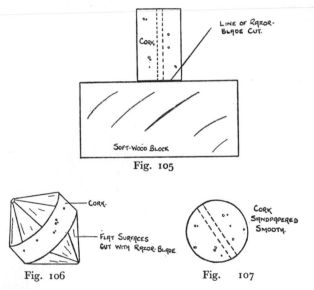

Fig. 105

Fig. 106   Fig.   107

In this way obtain a roughly spherical piece of cork with a hole through its centre (Fig. 106).

Smooth off all the sharp edges on the cork with the file first, and finish off to a smooth surface with the fine sandpaper (Fig. 107).

Next, cut off about $1\frac{1}{2}$ inches of copper wire and bend it into a simple loop so that the distance between the legs of the loop equals the diameter of the thin end of the prepared quill.

Place the loop with one leg on each side of the thin end of the quill so that the curve of the loop extends about $\frac{1}{8}$ inch beyond the end of the quill.

With the black thread, whip the loop on to the quill and carry the whipping on up the quill for about $\frac{1}{8}$ inch to $\frac{1}{4}$ inch above the ends of the legs of the loop. Tie off with a couple of half-hitches (Fig. 108 (a), (b), (c)).

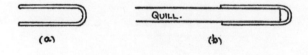

(a)   QUILL.   (b)

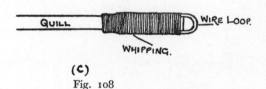

QUILL   WIRE LOOP.

WHIPPING.

(C)

Fig. 108

Now give a good coating of the waterproof glue to the whipping and allow to dry.

When dry, the cork can be slid into position on the quill ready for the final stage of painting. Dark green for the lower half of the cork and

quill below the cork is very suitable and any
bright colour (I use yellow) for the upper half of
the cork. I prefer to leave the upper part of the
quill unpainted except for a spot of colour right at
the tip.

With the cork in position, it will be found easy
to rotate the float between finger and thumb in
the left hand while painting, so as to get a neat
finish. Let the paint dry, and there is your perfectly good float for virtually no cost apart from
time.

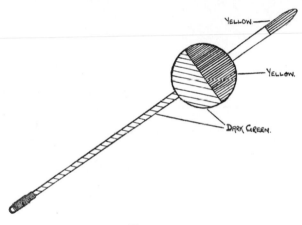

Fig. 109

A suitable stock of floats of varying size and
shape can be made in winter evenings in preparation for the coming season. I find them pleasant
and easy to make, and often amuse myself by
experimenting with various colour schemes and
cork shapes. The cork can be made egg-shaped,

G

rounded, angular, etc., and in various sizes to suit different types of water. Rough, heavy waters require a much bigger cork if a float is to remain visible to the angler, whereas in still waters the float can be delicately fished with a much smaller cork, and yet remain clearly visible. The eventual pattern of float used then lies with the angler's fancy and ingenuity.

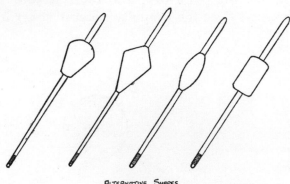

ALTERNATIVE SHAPES.

Fig. 110

CHAPTER 5

ODDS AND ENDS

Floating Flies

To aid the dry fly angler to make his fly float gently on the water's surface, particularly in the presence of any current, the fly should be "dressed" with a thin film of oil. Such solutions for helping flies to float can be bought, of course, but again it is perfectly easy to manufacture a suitable solution at home at a fraction of the cost.

A perfectly satisfactory combination can be made up using ordinary paraffin (the cheap variety) and vaseline. The bottle that fifty codeine tablets can be bought in is very suitable, being the right size for the pocket and having a wide neck and a screw-cap. Push into such a bottle a lump of vaseline about the size of a garden green pea and fill up the bottle with paraffin. Now shake and shake and shake—after screwing the cap on firmly, of course! Gradually the vaseline becomes dissipated in the paraffin, and, beyond giving a brief shake each time before use, there is the "solution".

In use, I drop the fly, already attached to the cast, through the neck of the bottle, so that the fly is completely immersed to the eye of the hook. Avoid letting the cast become coated with the solution.

It is worth rotating the fly several times in the solution by spinning the cast between finger and thumb before withdrawing it, to make sure the fly hackles all receive a coating of solution.

Remove the fly and flick it in the air a few times, holding the cast about 2 inches to 3 inches from the fly, and then make several false casts with the rod so as to shake off all excess solution and evaporate the paraffin. The end result is a fine film of vaseline all over the fly and the fly floats beautifully. If, on finally casting the fly, it lands on the water and becomes surrounded by a multi-coloured film of oil radiating out from it, then it means the fly needs further flicking to remove excess solution. The angler soon knows how much to flick his fly free of the excess before use, and, properly carried out, the fly will float delicately with no surrounding staining to arouse a fish's suspicions.

Carrying Flies

The carrying of flies on a day's fishing can prove very damaging to the flies unless packaged in a manner to protect their hackles, particularly in the case of dry flies, with their stiff hackles.

A useful method is to divide one of those rectangular 2-oz. tobacco tins into several sections so that the various patterns of fly can be kept separate from each other and their hackles not crushed. Sections can be made most simply using strips of thin cardboard glued inside the box as in Fig. 111. This arrangement can be varied to give as many individual sections to the box as the angler desires.

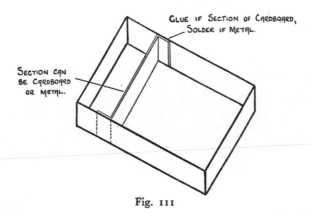

Fig. 111

The use of cardboard for the sections is satisfactory, but does not give a very permanent job, and I have used strips of metal cut with an *old* pair of scissors from a flattened-out food tin. Cut the strips to the same size and shape as the cardboard, so as to fit into the box with a short piece bent at right angles at each end (Fig. 112).

Make sure the inside of the tin and the ends of the strips of metal are clean and free of all grease; place in position in the box, covering the contacting surfaces with flux first. Now solder in position. Always be careful to file all the edges of the tin sections smooth and round them off,

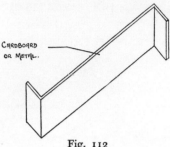

CARDBOARD
OR METAL.

Fig. 112

otherwise they can form nasty cutting edges for unwary fingers. If the angler wishes, cross-sections too can be inserted so as to give more compartments, though I usually find sections in one direction, about $\frac{1}{2}$ inch apart, give me an adequate number of compartments.

The angler may find that on a windy day, on opening the box of flies, several flies get whisked away by a flurry of wind. An aid to prevent this

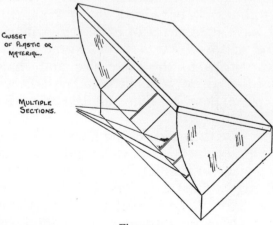

GUSSET
OF PLASTIC OR
MATERIAL.

MULTIPLE
SECTIONS.

Fig. 113

occurring is to fit virtually a gusset to the sides
of the fly box, using two pieces of clear plastic,
such as makes the little bags in which ladies'
stockings are sold.

Measurements will vary with the size of the fly
box, but the principle is shown below. The plastic
is attached to the inner surfaces of the box with
scotch tape or similar substance.

The plastic side panels are folded in to the
centre of the box on closing the lid, and they are
thin enough not to prevent the lid snapping shut,
and, of course, they act as wind protectors when
the lid is open.

Carrying Fly Casts

Casts with flies attached are awkward to carry,
and are best coiled up and carried in a flat tin.
Do not carry them in the traditional way wound
round the brim of your cap—that is, if you want
to have the cast in sound condition. Exposure to
wind, rain, sunshine and varying temperatures
makes even nylon deteriorate, and the angler
usually only finds out that he is using a faulty
cast when he loses a fish! Several wet fly casts
can be made up, coiled and stored in the same
flat tin, each cast being separated by a layer of
ordinary paper, since the wet fly hackles do not
suffer. Dry flies, however, should have stiff
hackles radiating out all round from the shank of
the hook, and I always attach the fly I intend to
use only at the waterside, keeping the shape of

the fly intact in the previously described fly box.

The reason for the layers of paper between each cast is that, without a separating layer, two or three wet fly casts with three hooks on each can produce a fantastic muddle, and the day at the waterside can easily be spent trying to unravel the mess!

Carrying Artificial Spinners

These can be usefully carried in a box divided similarly to the described fly box, but I have found the following arrangement more satisfactory:

The artificial minnows are from $1\frac{1}{4}$ inches to $2\frac{1}{2}$ inches long, including the treble hook, so that the reader will need a tin box about $2\frac{1}{2}$ inches square, and it should be fairly deep—about 2 inches to 3 inches. I found a suitable old tin, originally used for keeping anti-mist cream for gas-masks!!

Now cut out several squares of stout cardboard of the type that has a central corrugated layer (Fig. 114), so that they fit nicely inside the tin and lie flat.

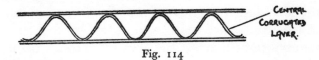

Fig. 114

This cardboard is ideal for lightly hooking one of the treble's points into, to keep the minnow from rolling about. Insert the point, nearly up to the barb, into the cardboard over one of the furrows of the corrugated central layers (Fig. 115) near one edge.

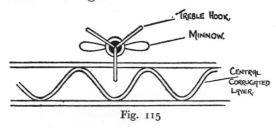

Fig. 115

Several minnows can thus be attached to one layer of carboard, as in Fig. 116, in a nose-to-tail arrangement. This forms one layer in the box, and I try and make each layer consist of minnows either all of the same colour scheme or all of the same size.

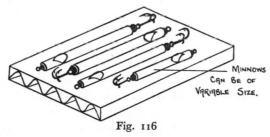

Fig. 116

Fit this layer into the box so as to lie flat, minnows uppermost, and repeat the process with other squares of cardboard, placing each in turn in the box one on top of the other in a multi-layered, sandwich arrangement (Fig. 117) until the box is full or all the minnows are accommodated.

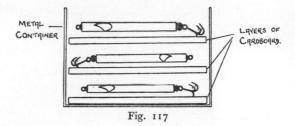

Fig. 117

The intervening cardboard keeps the minnows from rubbing their paint off against each other and hooking them into the cardboard prevents them rolling about and getting their trebles in a tangle. Not over-elegant? Possibly not, but extremely satisfactory in use, compact, and what's more, virtually at no cost to the angler. A box about the size of a $2\frac{1}{2}$-inch cube will hold something like two dozen artificials in this manner —enough for several days' spinning, even with bad luck!

Nylon Lines

A useful tip to keep your nylon line in position on the drum of your threadline reel is to hold it in position with an elastic band. Before putting the elastic band round the drum of line, however, tie a small loop of string to it as in Fig. 118 (a) and (b), otherwise, it is very awkward to get hold of again to remove from the drum, lying, as it will, below the rim of the drum.

Still easier to use is the nylon clip obtained on some 100-yard spools of nylon when the angler is buying his line. These clips fit round the reel drum nicely and have slightly curved-out ends, making them easy to get hold of and remove (Fig. 118 (c)).

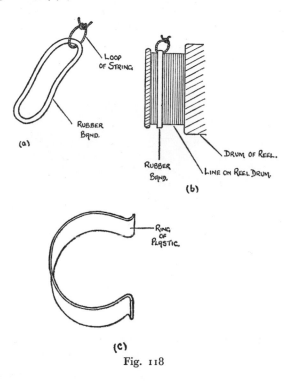

Fig. 118

All lines—fly, spinning or bait—should be taken off the reel and allowed to dry out after a day's fishing. One easily constructed line-dryer is shown below and can be quickly made from oddments in the work-shed at the cost of a few pence. It requires a 6-inch piece of $1\frac{1}{2}$ inch square softwood, 4 pieces of $\frac{1}{2}$ inch by $\frac{1}{4}$ inch soft wood about 2 feet long, some string, a few small nails and eight drawing pins!

Nail two of the long thin pieces of wood to each end of the 6″ × 1½″ square piece of wood so that the long pieces are at right angles to each other. For the second piece at each end, use packing between it and the central piece to fill in the gaps (Figs. 119 and 121).

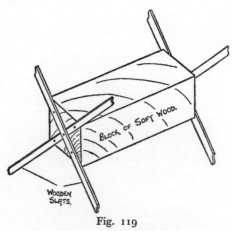

BLOCK OF SOFT WOOD.

WOODEN SLATS.

Fig. 119

Connect the tips of each long piece at each end of the central piece of wood with pieces of string, attaching the string to the wood with the drawing pins (Fig. 120).

To stabilise the whole thing, it pays to nail the long pieces to the ends of the centre piece of wood as shown in Fig. 121.

There then is the line drier. I pin mine to a wall of the work-shed so that it rotates and lets me wind my line on to it very quickly. The line, of

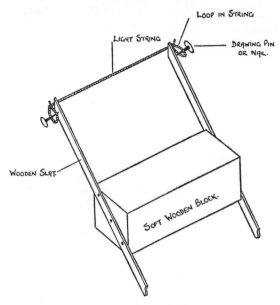

LOOP IN STRING

LIGHT STRING

DRAWING PIN OR NAIL.

WOODEN SLAT.

SOFT WOODEN BLOCK.

DIAGRAMATIC "EXPLODED" VIEW.
Fig. 120

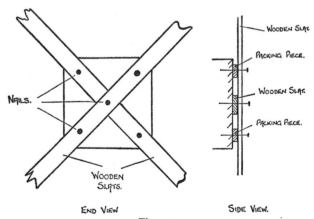

NAILS.

WOODEN SLATS.

WOODEN SLAT.

PACKING PIECE.

WOODEN SLAT.

PACKING PIECE.

END VIEW

SIDE VIEW.

Fig. 121

course, is wound loosely round the four string connecting-pieces and left a few hours till dry. While the line is off the reel and drying, is a good opportunity to dismantle your reel and dry, clean and oil it ready for the next outing.

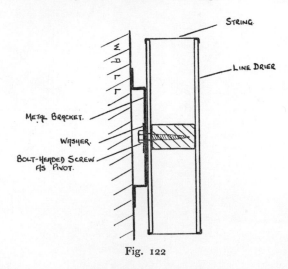

Fig. 122

Carrying Equipment

There is no doubt that a wickerwork creel is best for carrying fish at the waterside. Unfortunately, creels are non-collapsible and bulky, and gear cannot be carried in them or everything will get soiled when the first fish of the day is put in the creel! A useful way round the dilemma is to fasten a small canvas haversack to the outside of the creel. I've used this arrangement for the last few years, and find I have the advantage of a creel, yet a compact and easily carried unit which will carry equipment also. If the haversack has a vertical partition, so much the better, as then food for the day can go into one compartment and gear into the other!

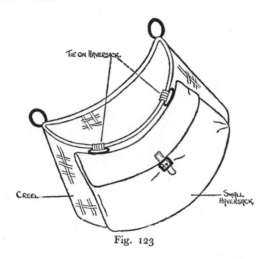

Fig. 123

Also useful is an Anorak type of upper garment. This is of light gaberdine material, showerproof and windproof, and has a hood and four large, most useful, pockets. It can be worn over the shirt in summer and the sleeves rolled up, or over numerous pullovers and jacket in the cold season.

They can be bought in Army Surplus Stores for from 10s. to 20s., depending on weight and condition.

Care and Repair of Waders

Good waders are expensive to buy, and anyone

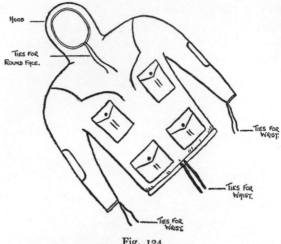

Fig. 124

fortunate enough to have a pair will want them to last for as long as possible. A point of major importance is to always store them, after carefully drying them, so that the "uppers" are uncreased. They can be hung from the wall so that the soles are on the ground and a string just takes enough weight to keep the uppers vertical and straight, or, I must confess, I find laying them flat on their side under the bed very satisfactory! and my wife seems to accept this now! (Fig. 125 (*a*) and (*b*).)

Leaks develop in the uppers at the site of creases and can be treated exactly as cycle-tyre punctures. It's cheaper to buy a roll of sheet rubber patching material 9 inches by 3 inches from one of the chain stores, rather than individual small patches. A sheet of material also allows

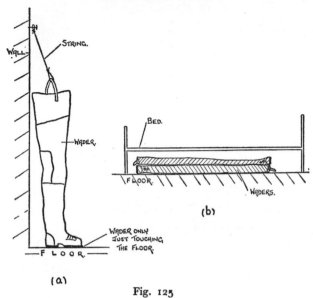

Fig. 125

the angler to cut patches to the size and shape he requires. Always make sure the wader rubber is clean and dry for at least 1 inch all round the leaks. The rubber can be roughened slightly by rubbing gently with fine sandpaper before applying the patent solution and patch, in the usual manner, allowing the patch to extend a good $\frac{3}{4}$ inch to 1 inch beyond the leak. Occasionally a leak is impossible to locate, and a sure but tedious method is to fill the wader with water and tie it to a wall or post so that it stands erect, carefully dry the outside, and then patiently watch for water to appear on the outside, at the position of the leak.

H

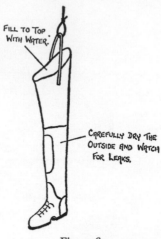

FILL TO TOP
WITH WATER.

CAREFULLY DRY THE
OUTSIDE AND WATCH
FOR LEAKS.

Fig. 126

Where to Fish

The young angler with his complete tackle outfit is well advised to accompany a local veteran angler on his first few excursions to the riverside. There is a great art in knowing *where* to fish as well as in how to fish, and it becomes much easier if an experienced angler is there to guide the novice on his first few outings. If actual outings with a local angler cannot be arranged, then certainly discuss the local water and conditions with an angler who knows them well. Much valuable and time saving advice can be obtained, especially if the various stretches of water can be studied on a good Ordnance map.

The following few paragraphs are diffidently offered, merely as basic guidance and can in no way allow for local circumstances or compare with the first-hand knowledge of a local angler.

In choosing a position in a river a fish has two major considerations:

(*a*) Safety from attack, and
(*b*) Food supply.

Safety requires the position to be either inaccessible to others or to be near to adequate safe cover, i.e. weed beds, old tree stumps, rocks, deep pools.

The food carried past any one position in the river is variable in amount, and obviously increased where water from wider reaches collects on its way through narrow channels.

Briefly, then, a fish will look for a position where foliage and nearby "safety spots" offer protection and one where food from wide areas upstream is concentrated into a narrow channel. The best positions for food are taken by the strongest fish with fewest enemies; lesser fish have to be contented with less ideal positions. Often a larger trout, for instance, will dislodge a smaller fish if it finds it in a more favourable position than its own. There is a constant shuffling of position among the fish population, due to changes in size of fish, local conditions, losses of members and so on. Obviously the fish's position near good food is also decided by the strength of current—larger fish can withstand stronger

currents than can the smallish members of the
fishy world!

With these points in mind, an angler is better
able to look at a stretch of water and mentally
note the likely spots where fish would take up
their positions. Obvious spots are places of
relative calm water behind boulders, where a
good current passes on each side (Fig. 127).

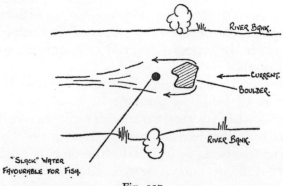

RIVER BANK.

CURRENT.
BOULDER.

RIVER BANK.

"SLACK" WATER
FAVOURABLE FOR FISH.

Fig. 127

The "head" and "tail" of rushing white water
are also favourable (Fig. 128) and alongside the
current's main channel.

Fish that feed on grubs and insects which live
on the riverside bushes will view with favour
pools overhung by bushes from which such food
drops into the water from time to time (Fig.
129). The foliage of the bush also acts as cover
and protection for the fish.

The deep, calm pools often prove uninterest-
ing to fish unless there is an obvious rise to fly

occurring, so that positioning of the fish is easy. The deep, quiet pools often provide large fish, however, and it is well worth getting to know the river bed of such spots, so as to know where the

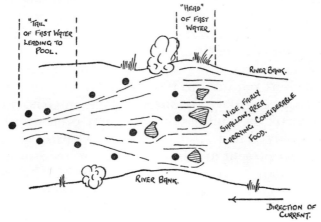

BLACK DOTS REPRESENT LIKELY POSITIONS OF FISH.

Fig. 128

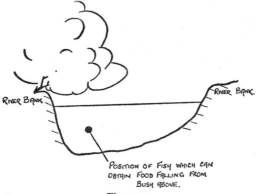

POSITION OF FISH WHICH CAN OBTAIN FOOD FALLING FROM BUSH ABOVE.

Fig. 129

food is concentrated; local angler experience is invaluable in helping the novice find the best spots in such pools.

It is always well worth while studying the available stretch of water on a walk along the river bank and making a mental note of those spots which look likely to hold fish, and yet which are almost inaccessible to the angler.

Such places more than repay the extra care and effort required to fish them. These spots tend to be passed over by almost all the anglers, and are virtually unfished in what may otherwise be a heavily fished stretch of river. Consequently, any fish present are much less wily in recognising and avoiding an angler's artificial lures. The risk of increased tackle losses in fishing such places is a challenge to the angler's skill in casting and a source of added pleasure when success follows, in spite of the added hazards. To follow several anglers fishing the same water and yet catch fish where they have failed is a sign of a skilful angler and, what's more, tremendously good for the morale!!

Thus approach the river and mentally view it from the point of view of a fish looking for food supplies from a position of safety. Having noted likely spots, *don't* walk heavily towards them in full view! Tread gently—a fish has a nervous system which is extremely sensitive to warning vibrations caused by heavy-footed anglers! Also, whenever possible approach the fish from a downstream position—remember, a fish, in order to breathe and to be able to see food carried down towards it, always lies with its nose pointing upstream. The angler, therefore, is far less likely to be seen by the fish if he stands behind it, i.e. downstream from it. Approaching in this way also lets the angler get closer than otherwise possible and enables a shorter and more manageable line to be cast over the fish. Remember

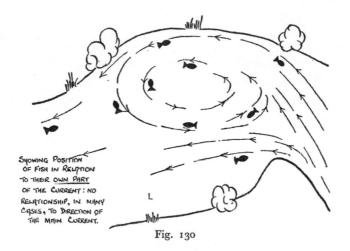

SHOWING POSITION OF FISH IN RELATION TO THEIR OWN PART OF THE CURRENT: NO RELATIONSHIP, IN MANY CASES, TO DIRECTION OF THE MAIN CURRENT.

Fig. 130

however, upstream to an individual fish means a "nose into current" position, and this is related to the current passing that fish, and this is not necessarily in the same direction as the main current in that part of the river. Thus in a swirling pool the fish may lie in opposite directions, each however, with its nose into the current passing its own position (Fig. 130).

Obviously it won't always be possible to

approach a fish from the "tail end", and it always
pays the angler to move quietly and slowly and
to blend in with his surroundings as much as
possible. A gorgeous pillar-box red shirt may be
the anger's pride and joy, but it isn't conducive
to good camouflage at the riverside! Fig. 131
roughly shows the field of vision available to a
fish below the surface—the good angler remains
outside this area!

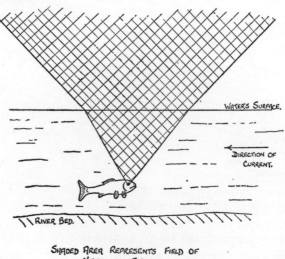

SHADED AREA REPRESENTS FIELD OF
VISION OF FISH.

Fig. 131

If the angler is having a day spinning and is
using minnows made as suggested in an earlier
chapter, remember that such lightweight minnows can be fished in all spots where fly-fishing
would be suitable. The minnow can be deftly

steered through the slack water behind boulders and alongside promising streams in shallow reaches of the river. Used this way, the minnow will be found to be deadly and also provide much additional fishing as compared to that possible with the heavy, more standard types of minnow. Remember, too, spinning is by no means always carried out by casting downstream and retrieving the minnow against the current.

The angler can equally well spin by casting upstream and retrieving his minnow at a rate faster than the current at that point, so that the minnow spins satisfactorily. Upstream spinning in this way allows the angler to approach and fish many spots, behind rocks, tree trunks, etc., which would be inaccessible if he was fishing in the more orthodox manner. These remarks apply equally to wct and dry fly fishing, the latter being virtually always a case of fishing in an upstream direction. In the case of dry fly fishing, the fly should be cast to land delicately on the water about 18 inches above the point where the fish was seen to rise, and allowed to float to about 3 feet below this point before being retrieved for another cast. Always place several casts over such a spot before moving on—a fish doesn't necessarily take a fly on the first occasion and may well do so after three or four or more casts.

In the case of wet fly fishing, the flies can be cast upstream over likely spots and retrieved in the sunken position at a rate sufficient to take up the slack in the line, as the cast returns with the current to the angler. A fish is easily felt on taking a fly, although such a "bite" is felt to be much gentler than when fishing the water in the more usual across and downstream method.

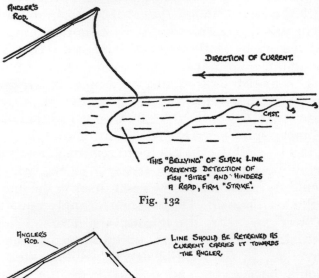

Fig. 132

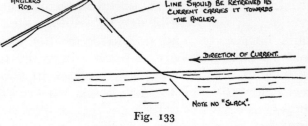

Fig. 133

There, then, very briefly, are a few basic points to bear in mind on arriving at the river bank for the first few outings. As the angler gets to know his stretch of river he soon picks up the finer points and learns the best and most productive spots.

Remember 1. View the water as if you were a fish looking for a safe spot with a good food supply.

2. Make a special attempt to fish any such spots which appear inaccessible and therefore likely to be much less fished.

3. Present your lure in as natural a way as is possible.

4. Where possible, approach the fish from a downstream position.

5. Finally, bear in mind that although the ability to cast a long line accurately is useful on occasions, the vast majority of fish are caught with short casts carefully and accurately presented from a point invisible to the fish. Longer casts will come with practice and are by no means essential to the successful angler.

Sally forth, reader, with equipment and enthusiasm and, apart from the sport itself, remember to enjoy the many other pleasures Mother Nature has to offer to the outdoor man.

Good luck.

INDEX